*For Sara, Mum, Dad, Julie, Gemma, the rest of my
family & anyone that's been subjected to extracts
from this at any point over the last two and a bit
years. I can't thank you all enough x.*

Hello. You know how Ryanair is the best airline in the world at deliciously petty dickhead moves? My all-time favourite has to be the part where they've just ushered you onto the plane three minutes before take-off with all the exuberance of a footballer welcoming back a torn cruciate. Then out of nowhere, they perk up and thank their frequent flyers like it's an emotionally charged Oscars acceptance, leaving everyone else on the plane blindsided and feeling like an unwelcome house guest at a wake. Anyway, not sure where I was going with that, but I'd just like to say a special hello to those of you that I somehow managed to guilt-trip or hypnotise into pre-ordering this book three months in advance, without all four of you, I'd not have been ahead of Katie Hopkins in the Amazon book chart for a solid twenty-four hours and I'd certainly not have been able to squeeze a poorly executed metaphor or another few lines of nonsense into this book.

RICHARD COBB: PART ONE:

THE EASIER TO DIGEST YEARS.

By Richard Cobb.

CONTENTS

BEFORE I START:

Ninety-five percent of my stream of consciousness in any given day consists of either trying to think up a shit joke in an attempt to cure awkwardness of a situation, when in reality nine times out of ten, said bad jokes will actually cause said awkwardness; or getting lost somewhere in my train of thought while attempting to conjure up daft get rich quick schemes, solely for my own enjoyment with little thought put in to how logical it is, all the while being safe in the knowledge that these ideas won't make the light of day, most of them being forgotten about and banished to the landfill of rubbish ideas mere seconds after birth. These ill-thought-out schemes range from waterfront driving ranges with exploding golf balls that were made from fish blocks so as not to pollute the water, whilst in turn feeding the fish (who I've since been told aren't actually that hungry on account of having a whole ocean worth of smaller, more vulnerable fish on the menu that they can chew on instead of a verging on inedible chalk like and smashed to smithereens golf ball. Even the fish would have thought that was a shite idea. It's like some nut-job running into Harry Ramsdens and throwing down some dry 11p Tesco Value noodles on top of someone's battered haddock thinking they've done them a favour. Still think I might be onto a winner with the vegetarian fish though) to an over-excessive amount of dreadful ideas for iPhone apps and accessories ranging from laser quest, a hob extension on the back in case you need a quick meal on the go, and finally a remote control fishing rod attachment with a camera on the end so you could steer it like a submarine towards the fish (who are probably all radioactive, if not dead as a result of eating too many golf ball fish blocks.) I haven't even fished in my life, so who knows where the fishing fascination has come from. By far the craziest one I've had though was when staring longingly out of my old office window in Sydney. The view was somewhere in between the Opera House and the Harbour Bridge.

The office view. (Credit: Angus Marich.)

I was neck deep in the sobering realisation that I'd soon be returning to Scotland. A Scotland that since I had been away had been diagnosed with a disease called 'Brexit.' I was desperate not to take a step backwards and fall back into the pit of another soul-destroying office job that I had absolutely no passion or desire for. With this grey looking worry cloud hovering over my head, I found myself devising another seemingly terrible idea. I would write an autobiography. With all my years of delusion, even I knew this wouldn't get me rich, and it would take me ages- so I use the term 'get rich quick' very very loosely. Then again, I had more knowledge and experience of myself than I had with fishing so it could have been worse. I put worryingly little thought behind the task other than the accurate assumption that when I would tell people about it they would instantly piss themselves and question if I was joking, followed closely with a "But why? What would you write about? You're not famous. Who would read it?" "I'd probably manage to guilt trip my family into it." Would be my response.

A late night train journey back from a Morrissey concert in Wollongong a week later, my girlfriend Sara was asleep next to me. Rather than opting for my usual time-wasting outlet of reading dull, beige and uninteresting Facebook posts for hours on end about people being pissed off with public transport being five minutes late; or an "obligatory" airport pint photo/ check-in, which I'd like to point out is far less "obliga- tory" than the individuals "obligatory" need to ram it down their ever-diminishing 864 social media friends throats; or an odd couple that I vaguely recollect might have gone to my school, getting engaged- complete with a close-up of the Haribo looking ring; or worse still, those that insist on posting an endless stream of photos of their child which people still fawn over in fear of looking like a dickhead for telling the truth about it resembling an uglier and more stressed out *E.T.* Tempting as that sounds, instead of all that, I began scribbling down a few ideas and moments that I could remember from my childhood on iPhone notes and from there I basically took this idea a bit too far.

So this project really just started off as a bit of a weird experiment without much method to my madness or thought towards an end goal (I'm referencing the book here, but the same could be said for many of my actions you're about to leaf through.) The more time I dedicated to writing stories down though, the more I began to shift the goal posts. What started off as a bit of a piss take, transformed into an opportunity to document the first thirty years of my life. Unlike my Mum and Dad who were three kids deep and accepting no further applications by my age (Sorry Mum and Dad, that sounded a whole lot worse than I meant it to!) starting a family of my own wasn't something that I can say I spent a vast amount of time focusing on. My big life decisions up until that point mainly revolved around choosing between Babybel's and Cheesestrings at Tesco. But (my old English teacher will hammer me for starting a sentence with the word 'But' but she'd maybe applaud me for writing a book, so let's call it a draw at this point-unless I end with 'and then I woke up and it was all a dream' in which case she fully deserves the three points) as I sat down to watch my favourite film *Big Fish* for the 900th time, I felt inspired to create a book filled with my memories and adventures so one day, if I'm lucky enough to have an uglier more stressed out *E.T.* of my own, then I can pass this down to them so they have a lasting memory of their dad, and they could pass it down even further if they wanted so my grandkids (Sorry Sara, bear with me on this-this is purely ifs and buts by this point :)) wouldn't have to shell out £90 for a tube to spit in so a dodgy company could tell them who their grandpa was. For anyone outside of that bracket that happens to be nose deep in this, thank you, and hopefully you find some of the following ramble relatable or even mildly entertaining.

IN THE BEGINNING:

It was late October; I had just let the cat back into my eight bedroom Shropshire estate. I poured myself a three quarter cup of Earl Grey (no milk, I've been vegan for all of three summers now) I took one final drag of happiness from my mahogany pipe, dusted off the old typewriter, sat back on my wicker chair, exhaled loudly, looked out the window for a moment and smiled as I reflected on my life up until this point. Alas, looking 180 degrees south to my somewhat over-bagged Earl Grey, I shivered as I recalled, much like my tea making, there had been some potholes down this long and winding road. This is my autobiography...

...is usually how this car crash shit-show of self-obsession would begin. I, however, haven't got a cat or a wicker chair, I'm writing this on an iPhone, I haven't a clue where Shropshire is and more importantly, I haven't really done anything of note that would typically merit writing about in this car crash shit-show of self-obsession.

Although the opening dialogue might suggest otherwise, I've always been a fan of autobiographies. The first one I read was probably a literary classic by The Rock, closely followed by Mick Foley's. The issue I've got with these things is that it often clouds my view of how easy it is to achieve something substantial. For example, after reading Mick Foley's book (around the time I watched MTV's *Jackass*), I remember thinking to myself 'piece of piss, I'll combine the two, become a professional wrestler and do mental stunts.' This culminated in a death-defying jump off my parents' old picnic table into some carefully placed boxes below for absolutely fuck all reason. I don't know what I had hoped to achieve from this. Although, in my head, I regularly worry that my life is one big *Truman Show* and that they only brought that film out to subliminally take the piss out of my situation as if it were one massive in-joke. Tangent aside (this book is one massive tangent by the way) I don't know what I hoped to achieve. In reality, did I expect MTV to be hiding in the bushes going "sorry mate, just before you risk your life, can you let us film it and broadcast it to similarly minded imbeciles and you'll have five minutes of fame?" Needless to say, that didn't happen. As I flew off the beloved family picnic table which had been in the family for generations (roughly six or seven years) the wind (probably controlled by that prick that controlled the weather from the *Truman Show*) decided to blow the boxes away and I just fell on my arse, breaking the priceless (£85 from Homebase in '95) family heirloom in the process. Is it a metaphor for what's to follow? I'll leave that up to the Advanced Higher English class that sabotage this book in ten years time, or the second year film school students who talk about how the cinematic adaption was the opposite of a feel-good summer film, like the evil cousin of *Sunshine on Leith*.

THE ACTUAL START:

My childhood was amazing. The four words nobody reading a non-fiction book wants to hear. Having said that, nobody's reading this anyway, so it's a bit of a tree falls in a forest type situation. Treetops, 15 Fergusson View, West Linton. Had a hill, a dog and until my sister Julie "accidentally" kicked the living shit out of Nigel Mansell in '96 on a late night toilet run, leaving a clearly distraught and shaken Damon Hill to drive around the circuit himself, only occasionally racing Thunderbird 2 on days when best mate and occasional Arsenal fan, Euan (I'll be referring to Euan with this title frequently throughout this book. He once found an Ian Wright Panini sticker in the garden, and I ridiculed him with jibes of being an Arsenal fan because it sounded moderately offensive and it clearly got on his nerves) was round, a class *Scalextric* set. I lived there with my Mum, Dad, my two sisters Julie and Gemma, our beloved Golden Retriever, Corrie, and my two teddies, Sammy the Dog and a red bear I named Custard (custard and jam were a lot harder to correctly identify in the early '90s, honest.)

15 Fergusson View, where it all began.

West Linton itself was a riot. In primary school, there was a three-week rumour floating about that the village was on lockdown after someone had been arrested for throwing a tin of beans at an innocent bystander outside the video shop one Tuesday night. No one could identify who the mystery bean grenadier was, what his/her motives were, whether or not it was Heinz or supermarket's own brand, and more importantly, whether or not it was a full can of beans or just the tin. Still, fucking great rumour regardless. West Linton famously had eight shops; a Costcutter, a newspaper shop, a post office, a charity shop, a book shop, a chemist (where each year I'd buy my Dad a can of Lynx Africa or Old Spice for Christmas and each year he'd act surprised and grateful for the thought that counts cupboard clutter), a fireplace shop (which nobody with an actual house really needed to frequent, so fuck knows how that survived) and my favourite of all, the local video shop. This place was great; it had everything you could ever want in a video shop; *Mr. Nanny*, *The Addams Family Values* (the difficult second film), *Indiana Jones and the Last Crusade* and last but not least, the stone-cold classic, *Mrs. Doubtfire*. How that place went down the tube I'll never know, but it probably had something to do with the tin of beans.

THE WHIPMAN FESTIVAL:

Every small village has a yearly festival; it's the thing that binds the local community together and partly explains its madness the other fifty-one weeks of the year to the outside world. West Linton was no exception; we had the Whipman festival.

The unwritten rule of having a festival in the first week of June in the Scottish Borders was that if by some God sent miracle it wasn't pissing it down, it would mean the midges were having a field day molesting people up and down the village green for merely having the brass neck of attempting to enjoy themselves under the microscopic sun. I can't really remember, and I haven't gone to the trouble of researching the main historical reason behind this festival (bodes well for the rest of the book), but the central theme was something about riding horses and wearing tight trousers, but I didn't get caught up in all that nonsense, there was far more fun to be had elsewhere. An early highlight in the week was the wheelbarrow race. The Lyne river, which ran alongside the village green would be flooded with sandbags and the crowds would gather to cheer on the senseless as they readied their wheelbarrow's dressed up like an Amsterdam hangover and proceeded to glide through the water with all the grace of a post-iceberg *Titanic*-minus the love story, before exiting up the bank at the other side, running around a cone, swapping drivers and sinking back into the water again, then finally attempting to get back to the starting point to end their soaking misery amongst roars of laughter from the unsympathetic bloodthirsty Roman-esque crowd. The fancy dress was always shrouded in controversy. For years the most ludicrous decision was awarding me first place for wearing a fresh out the bag Thunderbird 2 costume and best mate and occasional Arsenal fan, Euan the equivalent of a wooden spoon award for turning up, second place for going to the extremes of looking like he'd narrowly survived a house fire. He was impressively decked in the full fireman getup complete with a charcoaled face (looking back, this is potentially what lost it for him. West Linton council probably weren't overly keen on getting this printed in the black and white pages of the *Peeblesshire News* in fear of a revolt) and a fire truck that his dad had made him. One year my friends James, Ali, Jamie, Euan and I dressed up in kilts, painted our faces a more socially acceptable blue and white, wore jimmy hats and carried plastic swords in homage to *Braveheart*. We lost out to not one, but two Spice Girls impersonators who I'm not even convinced had actually entered the competition, they were merely sporting tracksuits and union jacks and wandering around the green looking furious. A style that would carry on in West Linton long past the mid-'90s and any fancy dress competition.

The Whipman disco on the Friday night was the night to crack out the bright red elasticated tie and the Velcro brogues. The playlist was the same throughout my tenure at primary school, presumably down to the fact that the village had about as much need for a DJ as it had for a shop that sold fireplaces. Girls would stand at one side of the room, boys at the other. Obviously completely avoiding breathing quarters with one another until the couple of bangers where everyone would lose their shit and congregate in the middle for a rave off; 'Saturday night' by Whigfield, 'Ooh Ah Just a Little Bit' by Gina G, '5,6,7,8' by Steps, 'Cotton Eye Joe' by Rednex, 'The Macarena' by, nobody knows who sang the Macarena, 'We Like To Party(The Vengabus)' by The Vengaboys and 'Spaceman' by Babylon Zoo. Yes, the Graeme Institute in West Linton was Ibiza like in the '90s, minus the drugs and credible DJ's and double the cherryade and shoeless sock slides.

Sports day on the Saturday was always tricky after the late 8 pm finishes the night before. Bear this in mind as I run through this next bit: As the main protagonist with an abnormally biased opinion for a child, I felt I had to be considered the favourite for the big one. The event to end all other events. The age six and under sack race. Assessing the field filled me with more confidence. I was going to walk this. Not walk it in the same sense that I walked the fifty-metre race earlier in the day (I was merely saving myself for the big event.) I carefully eased my way into the potato sack to ensure I didn't pull a hamstring or damage any necessary ligaments. Surveyed the thirty strong crowd that had gathered to see the '90s sack race equivalent of Usain Bolt. Then I focused my attention on the finish line. "On your marks. Get set. Go." THUMP. This hadn't started well. My technique of sprinting whilst in the sack clearly hadn't been as seamlessly choreographed as previously thought. Still, if another of my favourite films *The Goonies* had taught me anything, it was that a never say die attitude would bring big rewards. I got up again, and my momentum (or lack of) knocked me over again. It was around then that the tantrum floodgates opened. Someone must have tampered with the sack, put rocks in it or something. I was appalled. I was also still only one-metre from the starting line as the other competitors were soon to be crossing the finish line to a euphoric, if somewhat shellshocked crowd. It could have been worse though; I could have made it to the finish line by getting carried to the end by my Mum who had breached the security, ran onto the track like some sort of '90s version of Emily Davison, picked me up and carried me to the finish line, still finishing last. Oh no wait, that did happen. The horror. This was far from how I had envisaged my sack race career finishing. At least when it went tits up in a similar fashion for *CoolRunnings*, there were four of them to quarter up the blame and embarrassment, and they had a German guy clapping them over the line. I had none of that, and I couldn't exactly pin the blame on a dodgy potato sack. Though rest assured, I sure as hell tried to.

The scene of the fateful sack race.

The one race I'd always win would be the post-sports day five-metre dash from the green to the big lorry next to the announcers that would hand out kid's bags with chocolate and crisps once all the sporting for the day had been exhausted. I should probably point out that this was completely above board and part of the festival, just in case you had visions of a Scottish version of the child catcher from *Chitty Chitty Bang Bang* seductively dishing out the bags from the back of a white van. One packet of salt and vinegar crisps and a partially melted Freddo later and that would be the Whipman over for another year.

So that was my beautiful hometown and its wonderfully bat-shit festival. Now I'm going to jump back in the timeline a bit (this will happen a lot.)

HIDE AND SEEK CHAMPION 1991/92:

I was lauded for my hide and seek skills as a young-ster. Even in a room with seemingly no glaringly obvi-ous hiding spots, I would still find a way to outsmart my Mum and sisters time after time. I couldn't really describe how I became such a natural at this allegedly high pressured game. To my knowledge, I wasn't born into a family of hide and seek champions, so it was all a bit strange that I had somehow defied logic and self-taught myself to greatness at such an early age. Slowly but surely though, the wheels inevitably came off the invisible bus. I would find out in heart-breaking cir-cumstances when taking my one-man invisible circus on the road that my art of merely closing my eyes didn't mean that my opponents couldn't see me as I had once suspected. Turns out playing the same game but throw-ing in the curveball of trying to out-fox your captor in the form of actually hiding was surprisingly a lot harder than it sounded. The novelty wore off shortly after that, much like it would if an invisible superhero found out that they weren't invisible in the slightest and they've just been running around the city solving crime bollock naked the whole time, but their long-suffering, yet ever supportive superhero family didn't want to crush their dreams. Either that or they found the whole thing far too amusing to put an end to it. I should point out that whilst I can't remember the granular detail from my short-lived hide and seek career, I'm relatively confident that I was wearing clothes each time, so that's maybe a dreadful and alarming comparison.

EARLY ANARCHY/ PRIMARY 1:

West Linton Primary prior to demolition :'(

I'll briefly skim over the nursery days, I was labelled a prick for two incidents which myself and James (fellow hell-raiser) did, but unlike him, I couldn't talk my way out of them; throwing a shell in the swimming pool next to the nursery on account of it being next to the pool and looking highly throwable. I still don't feel I've been fully acquitted for this. It was clearly their fault for having an outdoor pool in the Scottish Borders. That shell must have been the only thing that had been in there in years! The second one was far more serious. Jumping off a two-foot stage and causing a racket for a laugh. I was essentially nursery's answer to Wolf from *Gladiators*.

I was once a proud owner of an orange bin lorry which did a couple of laps of the old West Linton Nurbur-gring in its heyday (prior to the ill-fated and untimely big foot demolition of Nigel Mansell.) That led to a very significant day in Primary 1. Now, I'm not going to lie and suggest that I remember more than about four incidents from Primary 1; the first being the old shameful classic of calling the teacher mum by mistake on a solid seven occasions (in the first week no less) The next being James (a different one) pissing himself in assembly and six of us being cruelly appointed prime suspects due to our unfortunate placing at piss point. The next, again involving James, when he "accidentally" put the wrong trousers on after a class dress up session (no doubt because he'd pissed his own). Anyway, essentially he was wearing my M&S classics (complete with name sewn into the back which was meant to deter such underhanded tactics) while muggins here had to stay dressed as a low budget, extremely pissed off five year old Spiderman for the rest of the afternoon until I solved the crime of who stole my trousers in what worryingly resembles a plot from *Wallace and Gromit*, but instead of the penguin chicken, it was, surprise surprise, the phantom piss thief who was the villain. The final thing I can remember and no doubt a pivotal moment in my early development was when they went for the whole "Now what does everybody want to be when they grow up?" chat, which I only recently cottoned on to was a way of the school preparing you for "growing up." Anyway, usual shite and thoughtless answers of "an actress," "a spaceman," "a footballer," "a fucking trouser thief" and then I get ridiculed by my peers for saying "a bin man in an orange truck." Tossers. If it's any consolation, I'm ninety-nine percent sure that none of them would go on to achieve their dreams.

Good riddance.

PRIMARY 2:

My somewhat tainted and unfavourable view of my classmates took a turn for the worst this year. Jamie turned up to my birthday party extravaganza wearing a denim New York cap, criminally long before it was acceptable or in any way 'fashionable' I might add. He then presents me with my present, which, though I was no Sherlock Holmes, Jonathan Creek or Miss Marple at the age of six, I thought looked suspiciously like a cap too. It was far worse than I feared. It was a carbon copy of the cap he was wearing that day like he was rewarding me with a replica of his infamous cap. I hadn't realised two for one existed at that age, now I do, my cynical nature detects that I may have got the free one. Nice enough cap though, got about three good wears out of it.

There was a hefty amount of heads down thumbs up played that year. Like proper obscene amount. Heads down thumbs up was a game that involved putting your head down on a desk, placing your hands out flat and raising your thumbs in the air whilst panic giggling ensued around the classroom. From here, three or four phantom suspects would sweep around the room choosing whose thumbs to press down, and then swan back up to the top of the class to await suspicion and finger pointing from the thumb police.

I can't really remember how long this game would last, but it seemed to go on forever. If you were lucky, it would be relatively straightforward to detect the guilty party, some of them would stick out like a sore thumb (FYI, I've skimmed back through this, and I can confirm that this is the worst joke in the book.) In the post-mortem, if you identified any sweaty residue around the thumb zone that wasn't there previously, it was apparent the blame lay at the one that was sweating buckets in front of the class. Some would cleverly try to throw you off the scent by deploying the frowned upon method of covering their hands with their sleeve before pressing your thumb down. It was easy to sniff out those underhanded perpetrators as they would be the ones with the jumper sleeves down to their ankles. I'm not sure what the incentive was to win, probably the chance to run around the class on a revenge mission, dropping thumbs as you pleased, but this was difficult to get overly-enthusiastic about given the trauma you'd just suffered through. To my knowledge, nobody in my class went on to a career in forensics or became a professional heads down thumbs up player, which is a shame given how much time and effort the teachers seemed to invest in this.

I imagine they play heads down thumbs up continuously in police stations to get criminals to crack and finally start answering questions because they can't deal with the sheer stress and mind-games involved.

The same year, we had a class hamster imaginatively titled 'Sparky.' Sparky was a jovial distraction from trying to draw a 'kicking k' or a 'curly c' with one of those irritatingly shite handwriting pens that may as well have been solar powered because nobody quite knew how to work them, least not near illiterate Primary 2 pupils. Granted, he didn't really do much other than look mortified that actual humans were pronouncing a 'k' and a 'c' the same and the only way these small humans were able to differentiate was to add 'kicking' and 'curly' in front of them after the less small human suggested that was the best way to learn. Nevertheless, it was fair to say the class was utterly besotted with this tiny bundle of fluff with legs. With the summer holidays fast approaching, our teacher arranged for Sparky to be shared out to anyone that wanted to take responsibility for him over the summer. From memory, three of my classmates and their unassuming parents had agreed to share Sparky over the summer months, like some sort of pass the parcel, though between the second and third parcel swap something went horribly tits up. On unwrapping the last sheet of paper the surprise was *spoiler alert* a dead hamster.

Returning for Primary 3, older, wiser and sporting a new *Jurassic Park* backpack and a pair of suave Clark's shoes, I plonked myself down into the classic cross-legged position. Our old Primary 2 teacher popped her head around the blackboard (we didn't waste money on walls between classrooms in my primary school, we just used blackboards) with an empty cage, giving out frown heavy sympathy stares to those in the know and exchanging guilty eye-contactless glances to those of us that were blissfully unaware of the shit show that had unfolded in the space of 6 weeks. There might not have been a hamster in the room but there sure as shit was an elephant in there. "As many of you are aware, Sparky, our lovely hamster sadly won't be returning this year as he unfortunately passed away at ... (not naming the hamster killer for legal reasons in case I've forgotten and it wasn't her) 's house. He'll be fondly remembered, and I'm very sorry children. Anyway, have a nice year in Primary three!" For years I wondered why I was a bit of a dick towards the hamster killer, but now having only recently remembered this turn of events, it all makes perfect sense, and it's clear why she was never vindicated. The one thing I feel slightly guilty about is that I was never really that fond of hamsters in the first place, I mean he was alright, but like I said, all he really did was run round in a circle on his wheel, sleep a lot and judge the class for our oddball tactics of trying to learn the English language, so to be honest, holding a grudge against someone for the fact the class hamster most likely died of natural causes was probably slightly unjustified.

The same year, Euan and I fashioned *Wayne's World* wigs out of the school's unreasonably sized wool collection and got an absolute bollocking for it. Being on community service for the remainder of the year, the rest was much like being back in Primary 1, but with less chalk outlined urine around the classroom and the majority of us had kicked our unhealthy addiction to eating play dough and PVA glue.

I'd like to say that my horribly one-sided love affair with music begun around the time that I got an Elvis gold hits tape. To be honest though, it more likely started before that when I was the proud owner of a *Power Rangers* tape or a Michael Jackson vinyl that I only managed to successfully play a couple of times due to my inability to figure out what on earth I was doing with my Dad's record player. The *Power Rangers* tape was phenomenal and a shit load easier to load into the tape player than the Jackson vinyl. My first glimpse of fame hadn't really panned out the way I had hoped. For the Christmas concert that year they conveniently "ran out" of key roles. Now, my class consisted of about fifteen people, and looking back on it, the powers that be could have at least had the decency to cast me as one of the reindeers whose name nobody remembers or an uninterested elf- there's hundreds of the pricks! I was instead cast as a Christmas tree. A fucking Christmas tree. I wore green and two of my class "mates" put baubles on my fingers. I knew my drama days were doomed when my Mum lovingly advised me "You weren't an overly convincing Christmas tree." Ouch. The Shame. Granted, I didn't exactly adopt a Daniel Day-Lewis method acting approach to it by sleeping in a forest for three months prior to the role. Maybe that would have helped. Last week when recalling the tale, she decided to tell me that when I played said Christmas tree that my acting would have been better if it weren't so "wooden." She repeated that joke a good seven times in the car, presumably in the hope that I would put it in this book. I politely completely ignored the request and volleyed back at her that she "wasn't an overly convincing comedian." Admittedly, her joke was irritatingly more amusing than my excruciatingly weak retort. Anyway, the good news is that twenty-four years later, I'm completely over it.

As an unwanted thrown away six-year-old Christmas tree, I knew that for the school concert at the end of the year I had to try to salvage points with a last minute recovery of epic proportions. This was my chance to turn the tables, this time everyone except me would be green (with envy, not painted like an unconvincing Christmas tree, which, again, I'm absolutely not still bitter about.) Now, *Power Rangers* weren't exactly going to cut the mustard, and the laser gun show I had in mind wouldn't likely pass the risk assessment. So I got one of those echoey toy mics and a pair of Coca Cola sunglasses then proceeded to epically confuse the whole school with my shaky leg dancing and muted singing over the top of Elvis' 'Hound Dog.' To be fair, I was up against it from the get-go when the teacher decided not to rewind it to the right place and had the volume turned up to eleven, immediately deafening my bewildered peers.

POST-FAME MUSIC EXPERIMENTS:

Music took over from there. My tape collection boasted classics such as; Hanson, Robert Miles, Aqua, Alice Cooper and some pish Mariah Carey tape I won at the Whipman disco for some outrageous *Karate Kid* inspired dance moves which I haven't been able to successfully replicate or better since. Mariah aside, I'm not at all ashamed of the music I owned. There's always a phase in your teens when someone would ask what type of music you listen to and if it wasn't already written on your black hoody or insanely low riding Jansport school bag, you'd strictly have to grunt 'Nirvana' or 'Rage Against the Machine' or you'd be dubbed a bellend. However, it's only when you're around that self-conscious corner and reflecting that you realise how absurd it is to hide under one small umbrella of music, particularly when there are hits pissing down from all angles. Unfortunately for me, with 1 in every 100 raindrops, there's a bird shit in the form of Mariah Carey. It was around the age of 7 that I discovered Oasis.

Sorry, I'll clear that up. I wasn't kicking about King Tuts having a pint with Alan Mcghee when they came on stage. I mean I was 7 when I first heard *(What's the Story) Morning Glory?* I was a bit too violently addicted to Pogs and cavorting around the playground in my Velcro shoes to have concerned myself with their first album. I had a Mickey Mouse drum kit and a love for Oasis, Euan had a Blur tape and an organ. The obvious thing to do next was to start a band. Euan, Ali and I were the core band members of 'The Moonshakers.' We had Jamie and Alan step in to guest on an album each, but we got rid of them due to a fall out over a bag of Monster Munch, football stickers or something equally irrecoverable. We were the closest thing to Beatlemania that West Linton had ever seen, in our heads. Now's probably a good time to point out that rather crucially, we didn't ever actually write a song or play any actual music. I hadn't realised that was a fairly important part of being in a band at that time. But the tape covers and song titles were phenomenal. We had an album called *Moon Dust*, and the cover was a mass of glitter borrowed from the schools unreasonably sized glitter collection. The stand out tracks that were not so subtly influenced by The Lightning Seeds and Spinal Tap were '2.5 Lions' '1 Lion' and "fan" favourite 'Rock 'n' (Bog) Roll.' I'm still worryingly proud of that title...

The Moonshakers- Torn Moon.

Since then, I've unashamedly dreamt of stadium success with a band, but I just haven't worked hard enough. I spent long enough procrastinating, seeing myself at the finish line but without putting the groundwork in to successfully begin the race. It was the same at school. I just couldn't hack the pressure I needlessly put on myself. It pisses me off as I find it difficult to put into words without sounding ridiculous, but I've always struggled when comparing myself to others. My sisters, for example, appeared to glide through school and university. I know that wouldn't have been the case and they put a hell of a lot of work in, but the general perception I got was that it was effortless. It's the same with seeing successful bands; I always think that I could have done that, but the reality is I never challenged myself enough to get to where they were due to substantial amounts of worrying about not achieving the outcome, sabotaging it in the process.

I asked my friend Kirsty if that last bit was too dark and she went "Nah, it levels the rest out if anything." So there you have it, seatbelts on because there's plenty more where that came from.

Eh, where am I? Oh yeah music, I'll get back to that in a bit. Another love of mine, for my sins, is football. You know when you love something that's really bad for you? Take smoking, for example, it's a one-sided love affair, you can be addicted, but it's slowly killing you. At least cigarette packets have started advertising how bad it is for you and you've got a helpline to quit on the pack. Scottish football sadly doesn't offer such a luxury. Match tickets should really offer visual red flags in the form of a short storyboard on the back of them of, let's say entirely hypothetically a hungover and extremely fragile Hearts fan having to endure what by all accounts should have been a reasonably routine semi-final against a poor Inverness team played at none other than your arch-rivals Hibernian's stadium. Not just any Inverness team either, a nine-man Inverness team. A nine-man Inverness team who it wouldn't be unfair to say were essentially bending over backwards to chauffeur Hearts into the final like an uncompetitive dad deliberately ushering the ball in his own net during a light-hearted Sunday afternoon kick about with his (lacking in ability, but making up for it in obscene competitiveness) son. Long story short- Hearts fluffed their lines, lost the game on penalties and the hangover got inexplicably worse.

Again, completely hypothetically of course.

HEART OF MIDLOTHIAN:

For the majority of football fans up and down the country, there's never been a choice involved in who you support; bar those, say in Kilmarnock and Motherwell- many of whom chose to roll their own dice, successfully skipping out the snakes and climbing the massive ladder to the promised land by choosing to side with one half of the old firm. This came unstuck somewhat when they released a controversially updated version of the game in 2012, which led Rangers back to square one with a distinctly new game piece, apparently only visible to the other players. I saw this path being about as satisfying as buying a pre-completed Rubik's cube, never going near it, yet still shamelessly feeling a sense of pride in it. For the rest of us, it was the family ties that bound most of us to the team we support today. My introduction to the trials and tribulations of Scottish football began at Tynecastle in early 1995 at the age of six, where I found myself at my first match supporting Heart of Midlothian

(Hearts for short, but I'm trying to up my word count here) alongside my Dad. For twenty-years I thought Hearts won that game 1-0 which explains why I was so keen to go back. It was only when researching for this book I realised it was actually 1-0 to Falkirk and I missed the Falkirk goal as I got distracted when eyeing up a fan to the left of me's King Size Mars Bar (which she didn't share by the way despite the best efforts of adverts around that time which seemed pretty explicit in enforcing this etiquette) and the Hearts goal actually went wide, but this was before my glasses days, so I went ballistic nearly sack race-esque face planting over absolutely fuck all.

Game two, we got absolutely savaged by Celtic 4-0. If goals were a King Size Mars Bar, Celtic were guzzling it all themselves without the slightest hint of remorse shown to the clearly starving home team. I wasn't too bothered by this result as it meant by the time the fourth goal went in we had nearly a whole section to ourselves which at the time felt like a great novelty. After the game, a visibly distraught fan gave me his scarf as he "wouldn't need it again." I've worn that scarf at every game since and it's witnessed three triumphant Scottish Cup wins. Still, not quite a King Size Mars Bar is it? A year later, I was the Hearts mascot in a game against Raith Rovers.

When I've told people over the years about the time I was the mascot, they've assumed I was the one dressed up in the dog costume running around the pitch on acid and minimal sleep, terrorising children and opposition players. In reality, I was just the shy one that ran on alongside the players. Even at a young age, I must have reeked of self-importance because I can remember running out and having a kick about with another mascot and the Hearts captain Gary Locke. I spent the whole time trying to show him up with my self-proclaimed footballing gift that I was somewhat shocked to walk off the pitch at Tynecastle that day without a modest place on the bench or a contract offer. I thought to myself that it was probably a good thing as I didn't want it to stand in the way of my bin man dreams.

MASCOTS

RICHARD COBB

School
West Linton Primary
Age
7 years
Favourite Player:
Pasquale Bruno

Rocking a turtleneck before it was cool.

My Dad and I, Tynecastle Park, 1996.

Gary Locke and I warming up.

In June 2017, I attended a Hearts auction which took place to help fund the development of the new Main Stand. I bought a few bricks and a seat from the now demolished old stand and I found the programme from when I was mascot buried under hundreds more at a stall at the back of the room. I took great pride in showing strangers in the room my awful photo from that day. I took less pride however, in informing them that in the twenty-two years since that day, its value had gone down from the cover price of £1 to the rather modest bargain bin price of 50p. A price so ego-deflatingly cheap that if Poundland stocked it, they'd have to sell them in two's to stop someone in the Leith Kirkgate branch kicking off about it being a rip-off. I also bumped into (saw him across the other side of the room and bolted towards him, cutting him off mid-conversation) Gary Locke that day and couldn't help but ask for a photo which I was keen to take up another half page in book space. I gave him a brief outline of what I'd written up until that point and how he would feature heavily in it (footnote to be fair) whilst proudly showing him a photo I had on my phone of him and I having a kick about all those years ago. His response was awe-inspiring "Oh...really? Oh right, oh yeah, I see. Right, eh...well, eh good luck with the book then." Narrowly missed the cut for a back cover quote that one...

Hearts legends reunited, 2017.

Shortly after that reunion, I wrote an article for an on-line football blog called *Talking Baws* on what the Main Stand meant to me. I spent ages on that piece, so instead of rehashing it, I'm just going to copy and paste it below.

'I've got fond memories of walking out to the pitch from the old stand at Tynecastle as a mascot in a game against Raith Rovers at the age of seven, witnessed by my Dad and my two Grandpas. This has lived long in the memory. Having said that, I'm still livid that after a good five-minute kick about with Captain Gary Locke that day, I wasn't offered a lifetime contract there and then. Today, I made that same walk out to the pitch (luckily there wasn't a ball in sight as my skinny jeans wouldn't have coped with any form of ball kicking leg extension and my ego would have taken a heavy battering at my lack of control) and breathed it all in one last time. I walked past the spot outside the executive club where I once had my photo taken next to Hearts record goalscorer John Robertson whilst wearing a maroon and white pirate tie, a cricket jumper, bright blue jeans and a pair of white Cica trainers. I shuddered at that one.

A Hearts legend and a fashion legend.

I've read hundreds of articles from Hearts and opposition players/fans alike over the last few days about how unique the atmosphere has been in certain games and the moments that stood out to them over the years. Under the surface of these stories though, there's a far deeper meaning. None of these great occasions spent in the company of the old stand would have meant nearly as much if family weren't at the centre of the stories.

I won't end on a sombre note, here are some of the pitfalls about the Main Stand, and some of the reasons I'd have gladly fifth geared a bulldozer through the place myself:

• By far the most insulting thing I've ever witnessed at any football game- It was Hearts defender, Robbie Neilson's testimonial match in 2008. In theory, the concept was a good one. The 1998 and 2006 Scottish Cup winners against the current team. What I failed to realise is the sheer amount of weight alcohol can put on your heroes in ten years. What I didn't fail to realise was how stinking our actual team was at the time. The scoreline was 4-3 to the new lot, but don't let that fool you, this game was utter shite. Ten minutes in, I sauntered over to the pie stand and was met with a quite frankly horrifying sight. It was the 28 Days Later of pie stands. Everything was gone. Not a soul, except for one quiet looking curry pie hiding in the corner. Out of desperation, I went for it. "Ach, that's not too bad!" I hear you cry. Wrong. It wasn't just any curry pie, it was a QUORN curry pie. An all-out assault on the taste-buds. Ever wondered why Mo Farah runs so far and so fast? It's because he's trying to leg it as far away from his Quorn filled fridge as possible in the hope that he never has to experience that devil food ever

again. Of course, this could have happened at any of the other three stands, but in this case, I'm very much holding the Main Stand accountable for this adverse event.

• The pillars and the restricted views: I've missed a countless number of goals on account of those pillars. As for the restricted views, I was so far to the side of the Main Stand when Hearts played Tottenham Hotspur in the Europa League Qualifying match in 2011 that I left thinking Spurs had only narrowly defeated us 4-0 and we were set for a showdown in the replay... Turns out when Gareth Bale rounded Kello he didn't balloon it into row z as I'd assumed, he fired it into the empty net.

• There's always that one guy at a football match, no matter where you are, could be a local park with seven people watching or it could be the San Siro, there's always going to be that one mouthy individual at a game that always gets the words wrong and generally makes a complete tit of themself. A few seats along from me one season in the Main Stand, we had the lovechild of Ian Beale and Ian Brown. Ian Beale in image, Ian Brown in demeanour. The season Hearts skooshed the Championship, this guy still managed to complain about everything from an accidental windswept throw-in, to failing to get an eleventh goal against Cowdenbeath, which in his eyes would have almost definitely put the game beyond all doubt. We may have won the league, but by far my favourite moment of that season was when that guy lost his voice twenty-minutes into game against Rangers when trying to noise-up the away fans, who were about five sections away, and too pre-occupied in trying to cheer up a then sixty-four-year-old Kenny Miller

to notice his now noiseless existence. Sadly, the prick got it back two weeks later.

To the untrained eye, it's little more than an ageing assortment of bricks, wood, iron, and concrete. To those with a football-shaped brain like myself, however, it's much, much more than that. Great memories are housed in every single one of those bricks and the place simply won't be the same without it. With the news of the stadium redevelopment being on the horizon for years, it feels a little unsettling that at 3 pm tomorrow afternoon at home to Aberdeen, the old lady will take her final bow as the curtain closes on what has become a landmark sight to the club and its supporters over the last one hundred or so years. The memories will live on though, and the new stand will no doubt create new memories for the next generation of Heart of Midlothian supporters and their families.'

I still agree with most of what was written above, though I've since developed a new found respect for Quorn (not just because they may or may not be clients of the company I currently work for and I'm trying to avoid legal implications.)

Grandpa Cobb, Dad, Grandpa Paterson and I with the Scottish Cup, 1998. The first of many.

My Dad and I, Tynecastle Park, 2017.

KERBY:

Kerby was a part fine art/part physics strategy game based on chucking a ball at a kerb, stressing out for a few seconds and hoping it would bounce back in your direction so you could catch it and feel beyond smug about it. What I liked about the game, aside from the minimal rules to memorise, was that whilst it was immensely competitive and led to many a disgruntled loser, the game was solely reliant on your own accuracy. So basically, if you mucked up, it was your fault and nobody else's (the novelty of this mindset would wear off later when I get to the bit about school exams...) The concept was so incredibly simple that it had never occurred to me that this game was being played anywhere other than our bubble of Fergusson View. Before the world was diagnosed with the all-seeing eye of the internet, it didn't seem far-fetched at the time to think that this game had been created on my street. I mean, it probably should have when I consider that my sisters and Claire, the next door neighbour-who I considered were the brains behind the operation, once tried to set up a phone line between our houses. Not using phones, using two plastic cups and a heroic amount of string (not sourced from the school's unreasonably sized wool collection I might add) which stretched about twenty-feet, high over the garden fence and through the second-floor windows into each house, then were crestfallen when their idea didn't work. Not everyone was as taken with kerby as we were, one of our arch-nemesis neighbours wasn't too thrilled that my questionable aim and misplaced enthusiasm would carry the ball into their garden and perilously close to their plants. Because I'm now fast approaching boring age, their pissed off-ness seems perfectly reasonable now, but at the time, seeing them as anything other than grumpy gits and party poopers was harder than smashing a ball off a kerb twice in a row.

As my sisters got older, the great sport of kerby got put back on the shelf, and one day we wouldn't realise it, but that would be the last time we'd play it. All great things must come to an end though, and it paved (shit pun intended) the way for football and racing around the street on my bike like a maniac. It would be another fifteen years or so before I twigged that we weren't the Christopher Columbus' of kerby, and it had been around for ages. I'm glad though because it would have been a travesty for no one else to have experienced such a glorious game. Hopefully it's still being played today and it's not just become a free app for square-eyed kids on a saliva-soaked iPad.

FOOTBALLING DREAMS:

Playing football became my whole life at primary school. I would play it every day for hours on end regardless of conditions. Each Saturday at 11 am I'd attend Saturday morning football practice at the local pitch around the corner from the school. I'd get there around 10 am to clean my boots and put myself through an extensive warm up prior to playing. I think this started because my Grandpa Paterson had once told me that one of my favourite players, Gary Mackay was always the first to arrive before a game and the last to leave afterwards, so I wanted to follow in his footsteps. After practice had ended, I would go home and immediately resume playing football in the garden. My Mum and Dad had bought me a set of goals and I'd practice free kicks, penalties and most importantly, celebrations long into the afternoon. As I was always preparing myself for fame (see signed photo on the cover for further evidence...) I would surround the pitch with the garden benches and chairs so I felt as though I were playing on front of a stadium. The addition of a patio spotlight doubled up as floodlights for those late night mid-week fixtures I'd conjure up in my head. For free kick practice, I'd go back and forth to my Dad's log pile which was lined up round the side of the house, bring them over in a wheelbarrow and stack them up to replicate a defensive wall. In theory, this was clever, though when you'd regularly blast the ball directly at the stack of logs, the *Jenga*-like rebuild would become tiresome and manual labour was never really my strong point. Football at school was a slightly different experience. When the ball inevitably got horsed over the hedge into the green-eyed neighbours garden or smashed through the head teachers office window, a replacement was needed otherwise the remainder of the lunch hour was excruciating, and there was no chance hopscotch was going to keep anyone suitably entertained until the bell went. A near seamless replacement would be a tennis ball, but nine times out of ten we'd have to settle on a sizeable stone to kick at each other instead which was a blessing for the Marks and Spencer shoe department.

The West Linton lunchtime San Siro.

One memorable lunchtime, one of my friend's younger brothers came hopping over to us in a great deal of distress. He informed us that someone had kicked his shoe on the roof of the nursery. Next thing I know, the janitor is frog-marching me into the school cafeteria to face a wall for the entirety of my lunch break. As I was facing the wall, my crimes were read out to me "you kicked his shoe on the roof" like some

59

sort of pre-hanging chat from a hooded figure. I tried in vain to protest my innocence but it fell on deaf ears. Then came the public shaming. All seven teachers arrived back in the front door of the school adjoined to the cafeteria and began tutting at me and shaking their heads like some sort of reverse guard of honour. Finally, five minutes before the end of lunch, Mr Bruce, the janitor walked in regretfully alongside the boy that cried no shoes. Both apologised profusely for the mistaken identity, as it turned out that - Quelle surprise- he had kicked his own shoe on the roof (bloody good effort for such a small guy to be fair) but he was terrified that his mum would have a go at him if she found out, so he pinned it on an innocent bystander to avoid the wrath. I decided to be the bigger man (and I was probably dying on a Babybel at that point before lunch ended) so I swiftly accepted his hollow and rudderless apology, much like Jesus would have accepted an apology from Judas (accept it publicly, laugh it off even, but privately be absolutely seething at the moral-less attention seeking little prick.)

I can remember attending trials for the school football team and for two or three years consistently missing out on a place, which would be read out in front of the class mid-afternoon in the days leading up to a game. I was always devastated and this would regularly lead to tears until I eventually managed to make the team by Primary 7. I scored a goal for the team which I was immensely proud of. I can recall it being an absolute belter which caught out the Priorsford football team's goalkeeper. My friends and teammates would recall a slightly different tale of how the ball scuttled across the ground at a snail's pace before nestling into the back of a net poorly guarded by an uninterested goalkeeper. But, as this is my memoirs, I can confirm it was an absolute solid-gold screamer of a shot that no keeper in the world could have got near.

CHRISTMAS:

My favourite book when I was growing up was the Argos catalogue. Each year, a few weeks before Christmas I'd get the latest edition so I could cut out the pictures of the presents I wanted, add them to my list and proceed to burn them up the fireplace to Santa, whose I was reliably informed had white doves waiting patiently on the roof of 15 Fergusson View in order to miraculously piece the list back together and fly them back first class to Santa's boudoir. I never questioned where the doves came from, how they knew what day we were sending the letters up and why we had to set fire to the list and post it up the chimney in the first place. Must have been a bloody nightmare for those doves to gather all the bits without the luxury of having hands too. I imagined it to be similar to the end of *The Crystal Maze* when the contestants were furiously trying to gather all of the flying tin foil whilst being encased in a greenhouse, all the while being antagonised by an overexcited bald man with a whistle. Which to be honest looked solid enough, even with the use of hands and a glass box to contain all of the pieces.

Doing that armed only with a beak and an unforgiving Borders wind must have been near impossible. From memory, there weren't that many flamboyant bald men with whistles that hung out on my roof though, so I suppose the doves had an advantage in that sense. Stories like that were part of the magic of Christmas in the Cobb house that my Mum and Dad went along with so well for the family.

One year I wondered, if Santa got everyone presents, did anyone get him any, aside from milk and shortbread and a carrot if he didn't declare it to the reindeers? I took it upon myself to make him some presents one year. I made him a stocking for the tree and inside it, I put a homemade flick book and a portrait of him. Art and joining letters weren't really my strong point back then, so my Mum had to make the 'l' on flick book more predominant so it didn't morph together with the 'I' like so...

And my photo of Santa hasn't aged well and worryingly resembles a tanned Adolf Hitler celebrating his birthday...

One year I was high as a kite on three-quarters of a Chocolate Orange and a Curly Wurly and felt that was as good a time as any to try to beat my keepy-uppy record in the house. I got to a fairly respectable, near record-breaking three before the ball took flight off my ever bipolar left foot and careered straight towards the present Gemma had just given my Mum, a glass that looked like it had wine in it- but when you turned it upside down, it didn't. I'm sure it had a more street name than that, but I feel the long-winded description is a semi-vital part of the narrative. It collided with the glass, and both ball and glass clattered off the table-top to the floor like Sherlock Holmes and Moriarty down the Reichenbach. Rightly so, I felt absolutely awful for what I had done. I'd let the clan down and ruined Christmas, this was surely leading up to a deserved *Home Alone* re-enactment. It felt worse when no bollocking arrived, instead, some powerful words from my Mum that have stayed with me ever since: "The sadness won't take away the happiness of when I received the present in the first place." :'(Gemma probably quite rightly thought I was a total shitebag though.

One Christmas, I got the *Thunderbirds* Tracy Island which was one of the best presents I've ever had. Fairly self-explanatory, it was a model of the island where the *Thunderbirds* lived, complete with Thunderbird 1,2,3 and 4 (Thunderbird 5 was deemed surplus to requirements as he was too busy pissing about in space, serving no real purpose and saving absolutely no one apart from himself in the process- to make the cut. Basically, Thunderbird 5 was a bit of a dick.) Best mate and occasional Arsenal fan, Euan got a special home-made one that year. I hadn't put two and two together at the time and didn't think to question why Santa hadn't just saved himself the effort and got him one like mine. I would later find out that his dad had spent months making it, as Tracy Island's were like gold dust that year. For the years before the internet, this was an amazing achievement, because the scale and function of it was spot on. Being a bit of a shit though, I would regularly ask Euan why his didn't have sound-effects like mine.

Finding out that Santa wasn't real left me pretty distraught. Until then, my biggest disappointment was finding out that Uncle Ben from the rice wasn't a real guy and that my Mum wasn't the women on the front of the red box of raisins. In my defence, she did very little to disprove my theory when she gave me a box of raisins in my lunchbox every day like she was harvesting them herself.

In my eyes, Santa was as real as God, only he didn't divide opinion as much and he turned up to work once a year, God on the other hand as far as I was concerned had taken the last 2000 odd years off after working for a solid six days. I don't think I was sad by the fact that there wasn't a creepy old guy breaking in through people's chimneys, in a way, that part was a bit of a relief, as that would have been every bit as intrusive as waking up to find U2 had secretly snuck into everyone's iPods unannounced. I felt more bad that I hadn't given my parents nearly as much credit as they deserved for all of the time and effort they'd invested into buying presents for my sisters and I. Instead I was prancing around the house in a post-selection box haze, decked out in my still label attached glow in the dark *Lion King* pyjamas stumbling my way through an emotional speech proclaiming that Santa was a bloody good guy, and his doves did a top job as the supporting cast for managing to piece together my Argos filled three pages of A4 list that I'd successfully cremated up the chimney with footnote credits of course going to the firelighters, without whom none of this would have been possible.

I look back on Christmas Day with fond memories, but I feel bad for my poor parents, as aside from Ikea, Argos is the most tedious place to shop on the planet. A whole shop worth of items, of which only about three items were visible to the public. The rest were stored in the warehouse-though if the items would surface was really anyone's guess. It was a case of placing the order and then kicking back on the inhumanely uncomfortable metal benches waiting for about an hour to see if what you'd requested would find its way out of the catacombs of the warehouse or not. Basically, it was an expensive and extremely one-sided game of Battleship with the moves dictated by an over-demanding child who, as we've learnt earlier, was fairly un-shy when it came to the old festive gift list.

THE RAINBOW RIOTS:

Next up on my rapidly expanding list of not real dis-
appointments was the order of the rainbow. If I said
there was some heated discussion around West Linton
Primary about the colours of the rainbow, I'd be under-
playing it massively. This discussion made the Brexit
vote look like the semi-finals of the *Eurovision Song
Contest* in comparison to some of the fierce debates
we had about the order of the colours of a rainbow.
Nowadays debates are extinguished after a few seconds
by a simple Google search (or a Bing search if you're
staring defeat straight in the eyeballs and you want to
delay your opponent a few seconds of undeserved happiness) a brief smug exchange, perhaps even a shake of
hands and then filed away in the recycle bin of your
brain. Back then, however, it was a fight to the death.
I imagine things like this are very similar to the sort
of trivial head-scratchers that kick off holy wars. The
once every two-years a rainbow appeared, the class
would anxiously look up to the sky and about three

seconds in start seeing stars which miraculously distracted you and made you lose the order you'd just seen and have to trudge back to the picket line of your initial theory with zero evidence to prove everyone else was wrong. Someone told me once in confidence that the rainbow actually started with orange. They delivered their theory in one of those intolerably high and mighty sort of ways too. Instant dismissal from the discussion and Christmas card list behaviour in my eyes, I didn't humour their witchcraft long enough to hear their bogus theory on what colour number two was.

To settle the argument for myself some twenty-two/twenty-three years later, I just Googled (and Bing'd and attempted to Ask Jeeves, who conveniently no longer exists when I actually need him) the official order. Somewhat embarrassingly, either the internet's got it wrong, or my once, what I thought was, iron-clad point of view was glaringly flawed. The alleged order is red, orange, yellow, green, blue, indigo, violet. Rather than accept the defeat graciously, I'd like to point the finger of blame at someone else. Now, for legal reasons I'm not going to quote the song because that would be breaching copyright (according to Google...and Bing) so I'm just going to list some colours and not mention which famous song about rainbows it came from:

1. Red.
2. Yellow.
3. Pink.
4. Green.
5. Purple.
6. Orange.
7. Blue.

To make matters worse, the singer of said song even had the brass neck to deliver a spine-curdling line about being able to sing a rainbow in similar fashion to the banned from my Christmas card list individual that was banging on about orange being the first colour.

This was on par with the day I found out Santa was both my Mum and Dad. At least Santa had good intentions, this singer nearly incited riots in West Linton with her extravagantly wrong take on the order of the rainbow which the young and impressionable would take as gospel. The sound engineer, her manager, her parents, SOMEONE could have had the decency to politely tell her that she should probably double check the order of the rainbow was correct before she recorded that song, otherwise it could cause some people real embarrassment further down the line when the internet gets invented and one young, easily influenced boy from a small village in Scotland, who didn't like being wrong would only find out at the prime age of twenty-nine years old that he'd been wrong all these years and it would only come to light when he was writing a book and adding, what had initially only really been a filler chapter but ended up being a full-blown breakdown. And sorry to burst your bubble Peggy Lee (the super-injunction has been temporarily lifted) but you can't claim to sing a rainbow if you're merely blurting out random colours! To make matters worse, on closer inspection, it would appear that Peggy didn't actually write that song, it was someone called Arthur Hamilton. So now, on account of all of his selfish lies, I've not only had a go at half my old class, I've also had a go at the singer who it turns out was just the messenger. If it later transpires that Arthur Hamilton was colour-blind and was just trying his best, then I'll probably have to apologise to him too (after I've Bing'd his diagnosis to make sure.)

EARLY CHARITY WORK:

When I was seven or eight, there was African shoebox appeal at school. The concept was a fairly straightforward one, fill a shoebox with well thought out everyday essentials, easily transportable food and small presents, which would then be transported over and shared out amongst the community in need. In typical fashion, I forgot to tell my Mum until the morning of, so we had to have a quick panic scramble around the cupboard to find something that would be suitable. Once the selection process was complete, I put it in a shoebox, and I proudly made my way to school with it. To my horror, when I got to school, it was abundantly clear that my classmates had put a tad more thought into this than I had. Some of them were proudly holding theirs aloft, others were opening their size twelve and thirteen shoeboxes to display a teddy, a football shirt and what looked like a selection of posh soups. It didn't end there, some of them had even painted their bloody shoeboxes! That wasn't in the brief, yet more than one had done it, so there had to have been some conferring or a secret shoebox meeting going on somewhere along the line that I wasn't aware of. At this point, I switched on the fasten seatbelt sign and gradually commenced my turbulent descent down into the depths of my chair. It was then I began feeling on edge and more than a little uneasy about the mystery item that was lurking in my shoebox. I envisaged a similar situation in my slightly racially naïve eight-year-old (remember this part as it's definitely key to this next bit not being the worst thing you'll read in this book) brain whereby a fairly sizable African family would be sat around a bonfire at dusk having just received delivery of twenty or so of these shoeboxes (by the way, this was a Scotland-wide event, they weren't just loading a truck with a solid twenty shoeboxes from West Linton Primary and driving straight to the heart of Africa which seemed extremely plausible at the time.) They're all absolutely buzzing at what they've got and the shoeboxes fly off the truck until there's only two boxes left, in what could best be compared to a *Deal or No Deal* type scenario. They each pick up a box and shake it, their mind going into overdrive at what wonder may lie before them. One poor soul has made the fateful mistake of picking my box which was *spoiler alert* the equivalent of joining the 1p club. Carefully lifting the lid in anticipation and excitement to fully savour the moment...then to be faced with nothing but a tin of black eyed beans staring back at them, which depending on how long the truck took to get there, may or may not have been out of date. The part that bothers me the most is that I'm not even sure if they would have had a bloody tin opener.

BASKETBALL:

Now it's fair to say one or two of my ideas up until then hadn't exactly been as well planned as I'd initially thought they were. This one was no exception; in fact, this was a front-runner for the crown of the worst idea of the lot. I watched a lot of Nickelodeon back in the day and highlights included *Saved by the Bell*, *Sister Sister*, *California Dreams* and *Hang Time*. Feel free to Wikipedia the rest of them, but *Hang Time* was the show that inspired me to start (don't let this word fool you) West Linton's very own Basketball team. The premise of the show was an underdog high school basketball team going for glory whilst juggling the pressures of high school life and relationships. The fact I was starting our team in primary school meant we would already be a fully-fledged force and big name on the circuit of the Scottish basketball scene by the start of high school. When out shopping one Sunday afternoon with my Mum and Dad, I spotted a luminous yellow and navy blue running vest which after going on about it for a good fifteen minutes, I would soon own. This would be West Linton Basketball team's official jersey. The following morning I folded it proudly (chucked it carelessly) into my school bag and unveiled it to the rest of the team. The rest of the team at this point consisted of Euan and fifty-fifty Ali. I wasn't really sure how many you needed in a basketball team, but two and a half seemed like a pretty promising starting point. I instructed them to go to the same sports shop and scout out the same vest, and once that happened, we could begin the second most crucial part of starting a basketball team, playing basketball. I tried to promo the vest/official jersey in P.E. once, but I felt intensely self-conscious about showing the upper levels/cheap seats of my arms, so I knocked that idea on the head. West Linton had a new court which was located at the far end of the football pitches. In fact, it was so far towards the end of the football pitches, that we'd actually only gone there once to play basketball before calling time on the village's maiden basketball team. Aside from the court being a good twenty-minutes away from where we lived, our shot success rate being abysmal, only having two or three players in the team and not having successfully identified a plan for who we would take on, I think the main reason we didn't reach the slam dunk heights of *Hang Time* was because I was the only one that had an official jersey or perhaps more crucially, the only one with a fleeting interest in the sport.

FIRST LOVE/S:

Rather obscurely, I remember a lot more about the first half of primary school than I do the second half. The main theme I seem to recall about Primary 4 onwards was the crippling realisation which carried on until my mid-twenties that I wasn't very good with those of female persuasion. And by not very good, I mean fucking dreadful. I once proudly drew a picture of a girl in my class which took me a solid seven to ten minutes of crayoning, presented her with it (complete with signature and date at the bottom of the page no less, in case, you know, I got famous one day..) and uttered the eternal words that every girl wanted to hear... "Here you go. This is you. Sorry, it looks a bit like Miss Piggy." I can't remember what sort of a reaction it got, but let's be honest it probably wasn't great, and I can't imagine it got centre stage on her parents' fridge that night. She ended up moving out of the country in Primary 4 which I'm fairly confident was ninety-nine percent down to the drawing and one percent because her dad had got a new job. Once that ship had crashed and burned before leaving the harbour, I set sail on another failed voyage.

This time I was two years older, slightly taller, but unfortunately none the wiser. I'd recently discovered Brut splash on aftershave and wet look Brylcreem, so confidence was understandably high. If I learnt one thing from my first ever gig- The Spice Girls in Glasgow with my Mum and sisters, it's that loads of girls loved them. Apart from one, it would later transpire... I spent a week's pocket money on a Spice Girls necklace from a stall at the Whipman for another girl in my class. Denying myself a week worth of football stickers and sweets for a girl. This was a HUGE deal.

My ever supportive mates were bemused by my generosity, then went for the primary school classic put down of "You bought a necklace for a girl? That's a bit gay!" Fast forward to two weeks later when after carrying the burden in my pocket for two weeks like a worryingly less masculine and massively more nervous Frodo Baggins, I arrived at Mount Doom (the bottom of the school steps) at lunchtime. Seconds which felt like hours later, she was standing in front of me — Sauron herself. I wasn't going to mess this one up; I had a point to prove to my two years younger self. This was the moment. This was my time to shine. I'd been practicing the opening line for days, so I was more than ready to proclaim my love through the medium of a Spice Girls necklace. I would kick start the love train in my year and be worshipped for my bravery and romantic endeavours. Reality's a bastard though.

"Hi, I er...well, the thing is...so, yeah I got this necklace for my sister the other week and she didn't want it, so I thought that I... eh, well... I might as well give it to you instead." All delivered in about three seconds in a high pitched and out of tune squeal. She had a brief look at it and uttered the eternal words that every boy wanted to hear... "No thanks, I don't even like the Spice Girls." She then proceeded to drop it down a drain. Taking with it my pride and more importantly my whole two pounds worth of emotion! Two things crossed my mind that day; the first being that maybe if I'd dressed up like a Christmas tree before handing over the necklace, the result could have been more favourable. Secondly, I should have bought six packs of football stickers and some Polo's instead of splashing the cash on that dream crushing devil woman.

The drain of pain revisited.

PEER PRESSURE FASHION:

Fashion in the mid to late '90s was awful and in hindsight, tantamount to self-imposed child cruelty at times. Tracksuits or more specifically, shell suits were the order of the day. There was nothing quite like the gift of a new Lecoq Sportif, Sergio Tacchini or Kappa tracksuit for a birthday or Christmas. Nowadays they're heavily associated as the battle gear of choice for bus stop terrorisers and Buckfast connoisseurs, but back in the day, they oozed class. Everything needed to be branded, particularly trainers. Two stripes? Nah. Four stripes? Good luck. There was a strict three stripes or you're out policy operating in West Linton through-out my tenure at primary school. It was definitely a case of over analysing the situation coupled with an unfathomable fear of not fitting in at school that led to these ridiculous close minded stances on "fashion" back then. Having said that, that red and navy blue Lecoq Sportif tracksuit was a thing of sheer beauty, so to be honest, I'm probably somewhat pissing on my point here. It's the same now for a lot of people in my opinion, but on a much wider scale. The press and tv shows join forces to promote their vision of the latest styles and introduce subliminal peer pressure for people to buy certain things to fit in with said trends, no matter how shit the product is. Getting a certain haircut because you saw it on *Boardwalk Empire* or *Peaky Blinders* once is my case and point. I can't imagine anybody woke up one morning, looked in the mirror and was struck with a lightning bolt epiphany that they needed to get a haircut like that just because they thought it would look good and it would be easy to maintain, provided you were walking slower than a snail through wind under one mile per hour. It's all down to trying to shape ourselves into being socially accepted by our peers, although very few will actually admit this to ourselves let alone anybody else. Off on a tangent again, but there's probably a bigger reason than self-pride and dignity which formed the main reason why I haven't ever really braved getting a fashion chasing haircut.

I've always had an irrational fear of going to the hairdressers. Even at the ripe old age of thirty, there's something unnatural, unnerving and unpleasant about getting a haircut. I go in with big ideas for radical change, but then as I sit there gripping nervously onto the armrest, life flashing before my eyes (depending on how long my fringe is at that point, sometimes it's just hair flashing before my eyes, so it's essentially just blind fear) whilst getting strangled to near death by the barber when putting on the aprony bib thing (allegedly to stop loose hair running down my neck, but also suc-cessfully managing to stop any blood flow to the neck) followed by the "oh sorry, you might want to shut your eyes" moment, crucially the sentence missing from every single barber in the country as they brandish what's apparently water (it might as well be pepper spray given the circumstances) and spray about four pints of water on your hair and face in Chinese water torture fashion before finally mumbling a sigh infested "what you getting done today then?"

This is like the part when you're in a restaurant anx-iously leafing through the menu front to back four times with no inspiration with the intention of just upping and leaving but then the waiter/waitress/wait-person (choose your own depending on what's more politically correct when you're reading this) rocks up with a breadbasket. Or when the rollercoaster you're on has just begun its ascent, meaning your window of opportunity for vacating the premises has well and truly vanished. No amount of preparation will help me here as my worried brain gives my mouth the standard default answer of "eh, not much just a tidy up, in fact practically nothing off please.no clippers just the scis-sors will do thanks" then proceeds fifteen minutes of not being sure where to look out of fear and awkward-ness (a theme ever-present in this collection of words.) Can't look at myself- that's vain. Can't look at the bar-ber- that's creepy. Can't shut my eyes- got accused of falling asleep on the chair once and I've still never lived that down. Can't watch the tv because it's in reverse in the mirror and I'm not paying enough attention to un-reverse the image in my head into a watchable or sensical experience. Why they bother putting the tv on at all is anyone's guess as it's nine times out of ten going to be soundtracked by an off-frequency radio banging out '80s power ballads, Capital FM or something equally stressful. As all this is going on, the likelihood is that my hair's getting butchered like an *Edward Scissorhands* ice sculpture. I still haven't learnt that losing my train of thought and getting distracted at a barbershop is as safe as putting a chip pan on and leaving the room. Then going back in the room, dousing it in petrol and leaving again.

The only thing that could save me on these occasions was if another customer came in midway through the massacre. That guaranteed the haircut would be finished two seconds later so the barber had time to nip out for a fag before his/her/its next victim. Regardless of the result, at the end when they brandish the wing mirrors, I'm just all like "Oh yeah. Yup. Yeah, that looks fine. Good. Great. Thanks." with about as much animation and conviction as when a waiter/waitress etc. asks if your wine is ok after a taster when you both know fine well that you're only ever going to give one answer because you're so shamefully ~~British~~ Scottish and in this case, you're not the one holding a pair of scissors or a corkscrew. Wearing a tracksuit didn't really carry the same amount of danger, unless it was a shellsuit on bonfire night.

SUMMER HOLIDAYS:

Julie, Gemma and I.
(Lake Garda or Menorca I think?)

Growing up in Scotland, summer holidays were what you yearned for and were undoubtedly the highlight of any year. Two weeks of sun a year wasn't a guarantee back then in Scotland, and global warming's further shafted us deeper into the fridge of the earth since. So abroad it was to catch some much-needed rays. The planning for the following year's adventures would start almost immediately after touching down on ~~British~~ Scottish soil. Travel brochures and the token 'visit Disney' VHS would be the hazard in the way of the door and the burglar alarm upon return to the house post-holiday. In today's day and age, it's so much different, infact, the only things that I can think of where there's anything remotely near that level of planning are wedding fairs advertised at the SECC in Glasgow seven years in advance, Christmas hampers for 2023 and a pension. When I was younger, it was a chance to get a nice new fake football top (which the crafty shopkeeper would insist was one hundred percent genuine and I'd lap it up every time) of my favourite Italian or Brazilian footballer with an unpronounceable name that I could show off to my mates. As I got a little older, the customary football top was replaced with an opportunity to adopt the old classic of "yeah I met a girl on holiday. She was probably a nine/nine point five out of ten. No, I don't have any photos of her/proof of her existence." My first pre-overseas holiday memory consisted of an ill-fated boat trip in the Norfolk Broads where my sisters had two sticks of rock and I didn't get any on account of not having fully formed teeth. At the time I was outraged and seeking vengeance. Looking back they probably had valid reasons...

Early abroad highlights largely involve me spewing my guts up. On a famous ferry crossing from Dover to Calais, I was informed by my parents that I'd be able to get a dessert if I successfully finished my main course. *Man v. Food* didn't exist back then, so I had nothing to aim for and aspire to when wolfing down the last of the spaghetti bolognese. I've never been particularly good at the art of multi-tasking. The main challenge here being finishing my main course and having a dessert whilst sitting on a boat. Unfortunately that evening I even struggled with the single-tasking part. Survivors of this day will tell you that this is probably the worst thing that's happened to a boat since 1912. As I sat with the dessert menu ajar, weighing up a chocolate cake or the incredibly ambitious knickerbocker glory, without warning, I'd hit the tip of the iceberg and the spaghetti bolognese began what I feared would be the long and arduous journey back the way it came. In the end, there was surprisingly far less resistance than anticipated. The dessert menu, the table, and several key eyewitnesses were left splattered and emotionally scarred by what had unfolded that day. Rumours have since surfaced from one of the survivors (my Dad) that it arrived back on the plate better presented than it had started and with unconfirmed reports stating there was somehow more parmesan the second time around. The harrowing part that sadly doesn't get anywhere near as much coverage in recounting of the tale is that I didn't get my partially deserved knickerbocker glory that day.

In a brief stopover one year somewhere in Germany, Freiburg I think, I took things one step further. Pasta again was culpable in this unfortunate holiday recurrence. Gnocchi had been my favourite dish since a visit to Perth with the family for my sisters' badminton tournament. The night in Freiburg ruined it for me a little bit. I'm about as comfortable re-visiting gnocchi as I am listening to (*edit*- a band with a singer that did something terrible that I'm not naming for legal reasons, but what I can say is, since that incident, I wouldn't be surprised if said band lost a lot of profits) these days. Anyway, back to the night in question. Shortly after the meal, we returned back to the pleasant, if somewhat cramped caravan we were in for the short stay. I was pretty tired after eating what felt like my body weight in food. Even I would be the first to admit that I'd have gone nowhere near a knickerbocker glory that evening. So I retired to the room, no doubt midway through a tense game of *Cluedo*, a game that I regularly subjected my family to on long holidays. I shared the room with my sisters who had two beds on the ground and mine was affixed to the wall above them. I slept soundly that night, one of the best sleeps I've ever had actually.

When I woke up the next morning, I remembered one dream in particular really vividly. I leaned over the edge of the bed to tell my sisters about it, but I could only see Julie, who was snoring, there was no sign of Gemma. I waltzed through to the living room (or the main bit of the caravan) to find my Mum, Dad, and Gemma in deep discussion. I interrupted with my dream story, whereby within the dream I woke up, leaned over the edge of the bed and proceeded to gently vomit onto Gemma's bed. That was all I could remember about the dream. Yup, it wasn't a dream. Gemma woke up thinking my parents had put some strawberries and cream on her pillow for breakfast, when the grim reality was that I was the accidental Phantom Ainsley Harriett and it was certainly not strawberries and cream. She spent the rest of the night in the lounge, and I continued on with my brilliant sleep completely oblivious to the scene of horror a few feet below me. I'm a little concerned that I wasn't immediately the main suspect in my parents somewhat flimsy investigations of the Freiburg incident. They had no idea what had happened until I brought up the dream about bringing up the gnocchi. It was clear that they had retained minimal knowledge on how to sniff out the guilty party, which is disappointing given the fact less than twelve hours previously they hadn't exactly been slow to point the finger at Colonel Mustard with the candlestick in the library in what I'm now guessing was surely a rigged game of *Cluedo*.

There were to be no more 'spewdunnit?' scenarios after that luckily for everyone. I'm not going to list every single other one of my holidays, largely because there's so much ground to cover and not enough work ethic from the writer.

I'll briefly sum the others up in a few words. Tunisia '98 (actually scratch that, I was inappropriately sick after misjudging an all you can drink Coca Cola deal at a Bedouin feast, and I outshone the evening's entertainment with my very own interpretation of a Coke Niagara Falls) highlight being when our 'taxi' driver had to bribe a charming police offer with coffee and cigarettes on account of him missing the small matter of a valid driving license. The tour guide on the bus to the resort heavily abused her privileges by using the onboard microphone to sing dodgy karaoke ('The Power of Love' by Celine Dion of all tunes) minus the backing track and telling offensive jokes at two in the morning when people were either trying to sleep or look out the window at the pitch black nothingness that Tunisia had to offer at that time in the morning. In fairness, looking back now, singing bad karaoke and telling offensive jokes is how I've spent the majority of the second part of my life to date; so in a way, Sharon no doubt subconsciously left a lasting impression on ten-year-old me, and for that I'm grateful. I'd never do it on a bus full of knackered tourists at two in the morning, mind. Inconsiderate bitch!

A couple of times in the early years, my Dad would assemble the roof rack, dust off the Steve Winwood CD and drive the family down to Lake Garda in the north of Italy. Substantial memories of these trips (aside from the aforementioned ferry crossings...) are fairly foggy, but one particular moment stands out and is still something of folklore around Cobb family meals to this day. We were staying in a caravan situated between two families. The family to our right resided from the Republic of Ireland, the family to our left were themselves from Northern Ireland. Unbeknownst to us at the time, they didn't exactly meet eye to eye. One afternoon, Julie arrived back at the caravan wearing a perplexed expression. She would proceed to have what started off as an earnest, mature and profoundly concerned discussion with our parents centring on her findings from earlier that day. She revealed that her friend from the Republic of Ireland and her parents were struggling to get on with our neighbours from Northern Ireland. When quizzed further on the reason for them not being on the best terms, Julie replied back with a straight face "well, as you may be aware, her family are from the south of Ireland and they're all Catholic, whereas the other family are from the north of Ireland and they're Prostitutes." Much like a taste for red wine and olives, the source of understanding just what it was that she had said which caused my parents to roll about the floor laughing at Julie's proclamation didn't arrive until a later age, but when it did, what a sheer joy to behold.

Florida 2001- Great holiday and arguably one of the best. The only thing that may have slightly marred it is the fact that I'm pretty sure at the age of thirteen and being in America, I thought I was Fred Durst. Limp Bizkit, the band he fronted were in my eyes (and ears) the pioneers of the nu-metal genre. A title fifteen years later I wouldn't wish on my worst enemy. I had a red New York Yankees cap that I wore backwards (like the singer) for the entirety of the two week holiday which at the time I was convinced looked terrific, but I can now confirm that looking back through photographic evidence, it most certainly did not. Didn't help that the hat was too small for what I had previously thought was only a metaphorically big head. I spent the fortnight looking surprised at absolutely everything thanks to the facelift inducing cap. That was yet another New York cap to add to the ever-growing bonfire of inanimate objects that needlessly infuriated me.

BULLYING:

My first real experience of being bullied arrived probably around the age of nine or ten. I'd always walked with my feet out at a bit of an angle, roughly at the ten to two position (this reference works best if you think of an analogue clock, the comparison gets slightly lost with digital clock...) I didn't especially deem this as peculiar at all as it was something I had always done, so didn't understand what all the hoo-ha was about all of a sudden. For one reason or another, it had been picked up on and things seemed to snowball from there. Some of the older pupils at school would pass comment and liken my walking style to a penguin which I never really got, but it seemed to stick. It felt like not a day would go by without at least one person trying to imitate my now infamous signature walk. As most would be at that age, I became horrendously self-conscious about it and tried to straighten my feet as much as possible when navigating around school, but having very flexible joints made it hard and walking like that didn't feel natural, above all else, it hurt my legs.

West Linton was a fantastic school, and on the whole, I've got magical memories of the place, but being a small school of probably a little over one hundred pupils at the time, if you were bullied it could feel incredibly claustrophobic. I no doubt let it get to me more than it should have, it's unquestionably easy to look back through a microscope and wonder why I allowed something like that emotionally erode me as much, nowadays I'd have probably just shrugged it off and moved on without the slightest desire to change who I was, but that mindset wouldn't arrive for another fifteen or so years. It felt awful at the time, and it was a hard one to free myself from the shackles of, but my Mum and teachers did a great job at making me feel more at ease with myself and the situation, and over time I felt like less of an animal at the zoo.

I feel a sense of remorse about the situation because an event like that should have been more than enough to put me off winding others in later life (much like witnessing a friend throw up inside my acoustic guitar after Julie's twenty-first birthday party should have put me off drinking and playing guitar) but I've definitely jumped on the bandwagon a few times over the years and been a dickhead to others when it's been unjustified just to show off or side with the "cool kids", so to solely play the role of a victim here would be unfair and wide of the mark. What it has taught me though is that bullying was, and I've no doubt still is rife in schools, and admittedly, things could have been a whole lot worse. From a young naïve boys point of view, it's hard not to get caught up in the toxic wave of it all in one way or another.

Learning from the experience, reflecting on it for what it was and if you're lucky like I am, understanding that it's not really had any bearing on who you are now as a human being, I feel is the best way to move on from that important learning curve of growing up.

PEEBLES:

High school- or as I like to call it- the difficult second album after a by all accounts rather unsuccessful debut. For me, one of the biggest mistakes anyone can make in life is to take unwarranted criticism too seriously and let it eat away at you or force you to change who you are as a person. Prior to joining high school, the best advice I got was to avoid being a dick so as to ensure I'd sidestep a head flushing down the toilet which by the way it was built up, sounded like it was a daily occurrence for some poor souls. If someone had told me not to let trivial things get to me, I would have no doubt avoided a substantial amount of the crap that followed me around. I've always been highly opinionated (as if that weren't blindingly obvious in the first eighty pages...) More often than not, that wasn't a healthy trait to have in your locker in the opening segment of my time at high school. I'd regularly voice my opinion when questioning the nature of someone's anger or apparent offence towards others and that in turn would inevitably lead to me receiving a kicking. Being mouthy didn't help, but it all stemmed from a sense of unjust towards the weapons in my school. Yes, Peebles High School was awkwardly tense, to begin with. I found it an uncomfortable step up from the quiet country environment that I'd thrived on and embraced at West Linton. Peebles wasn't exactly a large town, but compared to the scaled down model set lifted from *The Borrowers*-like West Linton, it felt massive. Though it was mid-way through my last year of primary school, moving from the family home in West Linton to Peebles was a hard one to take. You always hold a special place in your heart for the house you grew up in, but it felt a really tough one to take at the time.

I felt particularly bad and upset that our first dog Corrie was buried under a small tree on the hill at the back of the garden. Corrie died suddenly at the bottom of the stairs outside the back door of our house one Saturday morning after I had returned home from football practice. Aside from a few fish and the class hamster, I hadn't ever experienced first-hand how hard hitting the death of a loved one would be before. Having a pet from a young age teaches you many valuable life lessons about love, loyalty and unfortunately, loss and it sets you up for the journey ahead in life. I would later find out that she was due to be put down later that morning, so in a sense, hard as it was, it was lovely she spent her last moments on earth with her family surrounding her in a garden overlooking the hill that housed many of our adventures. By leaving her there alone and moving, I felt we were somehow abandoning her memory. Which of course wasn't true, but at the time I feared it was and I couldn't help but feel terrible about it.

To soften the blow, we got Skye, another high on life beautiful Golden Retriever shortly after moving to Kingswood, Kingsmuir Drive in Peebles. As with Corrie, Skye had a huge garden to explore and run amok in, often taking her life into her own paws by pulling off death-defying jumps off the driveway, over the flower-bed and onto the grass below whenever she felt like it. She arrived at an important time for my sisters and I and would regularly offer us a loving paw in con-dolence or an uninvited face lick if we'd had a rough day at school.

Though I continued to attend West Linton Primary until I finished Primary 7, that mere twenty miles up the road from my friends felt like a considerable dis-tance. This proved harder at high school as I longed for the bus to and from school chat with my friends, but didn't get that as I lived just around the corner from the school in Peebles. I later learned that I hadn't missed much and allegedly the wedgie rate on that bus was mental, so I probably dodged a bullet as well as a ripped pair of boxer shorts.

To begin with, there was undoubtedly a great deal more shops in my step-town, though this wasn't neces-sarily all that necessary on account of the lion's share of them being charity shops. Now before you start, I'm in no way questioning the importance of charity shops.

Obviously, they serve their purpose and can really help make a difference to those in need. It was more the sheer volume of them and the fact that they took up about eighty percent of the shops in town that was my bugbear. It's fair to say these charity shops in question typically had mostly fuck all in them apart from a few odd pairs of shoes, a *Full Monty* VHS with the Blockbuster label marker penned out (in hindsight, this Robin Hood approach to video rental more than likely contributed in part to the demise of video shop culture) a *Blue Peter* annual from 1991 (with the crossword already completed) and a mere twelve copies of *The Da Vinci Code*.

Suffice to say; they weren't exactly Bob Geldofing the money in. Probably went down a rabbit hole I shouldn't have there, I'll quickly move on...

The biggest scandal to hit Peebles was when the Job Centre closed. Not quite as Poirot like as the tin of beans incident in West Linton on the face of it, but the plot thickens. The scandal surprisingly wasn't the actual closing of said Job Centre; it was what would follow that would get the community readying their pitchforks and wielding their torches. The building in the Northgate in Peebles lay dormant for several months with minimal activity inside (much like it did when there was a Job Centre there) until the builders moved in and began gutting the place. This would trigger Chinese whispers around the town about who or what would be taking over the vacant property.

One midweek day, out of nowhere there appeared a handwritten black and white sign that simply read 'Sex shop-opening soon.' The horror spread quicker than Nutella on a warm day. The unsexed and unsuspecting townspeople were incensed. I could envisage many a scone raisin and English Breakfast tea being half choked/half spat over the local coffee shop Ramblers tablecloths at this news. "S-s-s-secks shop? Oh, I don't think that would happen — surely n...ohmygodtheresasign. Mavis, there's a sign, a sign, Mavis, an actual sign. Grab your Zimmer and your teeth; we're off to the newspaper." Conveniently the old offices of *The Peeblesshire News* were located directly across the road from the new shop, so they were able to snap a photo for the front page by just poking their large Nikon through the blinds. That sounded much worse than it should have... anyway, after a record number of letters to the newspaper (probably about four) it turned out to be a hoax from one of the builders and the empty unit rather boringly turned into someone's house and not a sex shop (or another bloody charity shop.) Meaning the town could sleep easily again, most of them safe in the knowledge that they could continue to buy their handcuffs and gimp costumes online in the sly instead of being caught anywhere near a "disgoosting sex shop."

EGG CHASING:

The school had an overwhelming focus (bias) on rugby. In my younger days, I loved rugby. I'd always participate in the yearly rugby tournament in West Linton, probably because there was an easy route to a medal. I collected six medals at a sport that apparently required zero of my understanding. I was convinced that I'd beaten the system on account of having about as much of an idea what I was doing as I did when I used to play the recorder, which was less about skill and more a tool to get out of class without harbouring any affection for the sound that came out of the overindulgent older sibling of the tin whistle. I was bloody great at miming though. Rugby in high school had that somewhat crucial difference in that it was full contact and there were some absolute bruisers in my year who no doubt ate hammers and nails for breakfast and washed it down with crude oil and smaller classmates tears.

Walking out onto the field on the first day of P.E. was the Borders equivalent of Pearl Harbor. Rock hard rugby balls torpedoing all over the place and bodies flying everywhere. Suffice to say, this sport wasn't for me, and I opted to carry on with what the school considered the niche almost unheard of sport of football. That's maybe a tad unfair, but for the majority of the rugby-obsessed department, football visibly took a back seat on the broken down bus at the back of the line of their egg-shaped priorities. They even preferred country dancing over football!

Once a year around Christmas, country dancing was compulsory to prepare people for a non-compulsory school dance. Country dancing was my worst nightmare. On the one hand, there was the opportunity to dance with the girl you fancied at school, on the other hand, that never fucking happened and I'd always opt instead for the least likely and least mobile one with burst taps for hands in fear of rejection and looking like the king of the tossers. That might seem incredibly shallow, and it is, but that was high school for you, shallower than the shallowest of shallow ends of a child's shallow pool that's had all its water drained out. Being prime wedding age now, it's clear that a freakish amount of people have actually retained some knowledge from this scarring time in our lives. I remembered none of it, aside from the tap hands of course.

THE COBBIT:

That year, 2001 I saw *The Lord of the Rings* at the cinema with my Dad. I loved these films and each year I'd get the extended editions on DVD for Christmas and watch the 700 hour extra features which featured something like a twenty-five minute interview with a dull as dishwater cross-eyed art director who filmed a model tree non-stop for a week and then bored the tits off everyone when explaining it in granular detail. I lapped this shit up though, the two bonus discs of fuck all were the highlights of my year over those three years. For the next three years, I momentarily put my bin man dreams on ice, and all I wanted to be was a film director, Scotland's answer to Peter Jackson. Yet again I felt sure this was to be my route to fame. All that went wrong was that the only original idea I had for a film wasn't original at all, I wanted to remake *The Lord of the Rings* with no cast, no camera, no budget, no car to get me to the locations that I'd seen when I'd driven past them with my parents and somewhat crucially, no ring!

It took me three years to realise there was absolutely no point in this and no prospect of this idea making it out of my Hobbit sized Peebles bedroom. So effectively, like many of my ill thought out schemes, the dream died before it could even be arsed to be born. I visited the Hobbiton set with Sara when we went to New Zealand in 2016, and it reignited my desire to make films again, then I remembered my original predicament of still only having one idea for a film and by that point Peter Jackson had made six of the fuckers so the copyright lawsuit would probably not have been on my side. Not to mention, I still had no cast, no camera, no budget and whilst I had a car, more crucially, much to my hat-loving Mum's disappointment, I still had no ring.

Sara and I visit Hobbiton, New Zealand, August 2016.

S.S.S.SEEX EDUCATION:

Without going into too much detail, my early to mid-teen years were a bit like a budget *American Pie* meets *The Exorcist*. Hormones had that crippling effect of one day having zero understanding or care for literally the ins and outs of sex to the next turning into a low on self-esteem, lower on chat, closet Russell Brand minus the bedpost notches and luscious locks. For the benefit of anyone lucky enough to be unaware of what it was like, imagine an over-exuberant puppy wanting to latch itself on to anything that moved and you'll not be far off the mark. I'm convinced that the first couple of years of high school were so tricky for a lot of people, because every red-blooded male between the ages of thirteen and sixteen was impacted by what was essentially teen wolf syndrome and it caused most of us to be, though somewhat unintentionally, complete arseholes ninety-nine percent of the time. Obviously, it impacted females too in different ways, but I can only speak for myself through the experience of being one of those intolerable and needlessly sour-faced wankers.

It's one of those things that's difficult to make sense of or come to terms with at the time, but it was definitely a burden for a lot of people when looking back on it. One of the main issues is that it's a grey area in which the education system in the UK doesn't really know how to tackle either, like religion. Both are such sensitive subjects that they tend to tip-toe around the subjects with a verging on medieval approach so as not to offend anyone instead of tackling the important issues head-on. It doesn't help that the room is lost to irreconcilable laughter when folk start shouting out "cock and balls" five minutes into the section about slang terms. In Sex Education that is, this didn't really happen as much in R.E ...

I think in order for this stigma and awkwardness towards the subject to go away, all it really needs is a modernised and approachable support network that covers and truly understands the psychological predicament that teenagers are in. The coverage was iceberg-like, to say the least in that it ticked off most of the obvious stuff ("that goes in there") but there was far more beneath the surface for people to deal with and it dare not comprehend the mindset of the pupils experiencing physical and mental changes on account of a long and perilously uncomfortable journey across the rickety bridge from childhood into being an adult, a journey that's hidden in the small print of the terms and conditions of being a teenager. More shockingly in my eyes, no mention was made of anything other than relationships between a man and a woman, which could have made it easier for many of my schoolmates who didn't come out until leaving the incredibly claustrophobic surroundings of high school. Whilst support was there, it never really felt accessible or an option for young people to take seriously in order to fully understand the reason behind being ill at ease with themselves and the changes they were going through at the time. This isn't by any means a dig solely at the high school I went to, it's schools up and down the country that adopted this half-arsed approach. If it's nipped in the bud at schools, then it could open doors to other platforms like professional footballers, for example, to feel more comfortable in their own skin without fear of backlash against them in the future. If there wasn't a stigma attached or a cloud surrounding it, there would be nothing to be made fun of and everyone could eat

Skittles together from the bowl of happiness.

HOME ECONOMICS:

Home Economics was savage in first year too. Needing to pay a few pounds of my parents' money for ingredients prior to the weekly bake day was torture on the soul and I genuinely felt awful at asking my parents for the money as I knew the only return they'd get on their investment would be salmonella or best case mild stomach trauma for a week. Whilst some other pupils would make *Bake Off*-esque cakes for their Mum who upon receiving them was no doubt too proud as punch to eat them on account of how immaculate they looked; and instead probably opted to mummify them and add them to her patisserie pyramid of pride in the cabinet in their hallway in order to show them off to her equally painfully smug Stepford Wife friends. I, on the other hand, would be hoping for a sudden gust of wind on the five minute journey home that would fly my accidentally too literal rock buns straight to the bottom of the sea, with any luck taking out the decent cakes on their flight path. As if my cooking ability wasn't enough suffering, I had a frighteningly tall teacher whose name escapes me, but her nickname of "Big Bird" was wonderfully accurate, if more than just a little offensive. My lasting memory of her classes centred around me getting a Gordon Ramsay inspired barrage of abuse (bollocking, some would say) from her one fateful afternoon for incorrectly identifying a tablespoon from a pile of about four-hundred spoons, nearly resulting in an onion chopping reaction from my eyes in front of my fear-filled classmates, who I'm guessing had the same level of spoon knowledge as she had decorum. Still, I don't hold it against her for that outburst. It must have been hard having such a great job over the years where loads of kids looked up to you, and then having to leave it all behind and move out of *Sesame Street* to become a full-time Home Economics teacher with an unhealthy spoon infatuation.

FIRST LOVE/S PT II:

Relationships in the first few years of high school are wonderful to look back on, in the same way that falling arse first through a swing door of a sports hall cafeteria at the age of eight during a lunch break at one of my sisters' tennis tournaments in front of a capacity crowd of unsympathetic wankers is wonderful to look back on. The post-mortem fifteen years later can identify two main causes for the end of the world feeling that the demise of your first relationship would bring. Number 1) self-doubt and melodrama. The feeling that you'd be sad for the rest of your life was partially brought on by culprit number 2) Coldplay. Coldplay were the pioneers of a sad song back then. 'Trouble,' 'The Scientist,' and 'Fix You' made even R.E.M. look like The Village People. I don't mind Coldplay, but they definitely made the end of a four-week "relationship" feel like the end of *The Notebook* or *Four Weddings and a Funeral*, if there were no weddings-just one massive self-indulgent funeral with only the victim in attendance. High school was basically just one enormous pantomime. Obviously at the time heartbreak can feel a thousand times worse and it can understandably be a hard one to take, it just seems

so laughable now when I think about it as I'm struggling to find anything remotely romantic about a first
(and coincidentally yet unsurprisingly last) date. The
big date consisted of a forty minute round trip by foot
to the Scotmid on a Saturday afternoon to individually
purchase roughly £3 of pick 'n' mix before hot-footing
it back down the road sugared off our tits but seriously
struggling in the art of conversation when it came to
talking about anything other than the familiar texture
of 4p big strawberries or cola bottles. Maybe things
would have worked out differently had I paid for her
pick 'n' mix that day, but clearly, I must have sensed all
was not well, and I wasn't prepared to get burned for
£3 in a more expensive repeat performance of the now
infamous Spice Girls necklace failure two years previously. Absolute masterstroke in foresight now I think
about it. The £3 saved would be just enough to buy
Coldplay's new single 'Trouble.' Every cloud...

I had another short-lived gondola ride down the canal
of love (that's not a euphemism) a couple of months
after that. Rather cleverly I'd set the benchmark so im-
possibly low last time, that the next surely couldn't
have gone any worse. Well... sort of. By all accounts,
this had a slightly longer shelf-life, but as you'll quickly
learn, in some cases that's not necessarily a good thing.
For example, powdered milk's got a longer shelf-life
than semi-skimmed, it may not go as sour but it re-
quires a lot more effort and it's difficult to stomach at
the best of times. For her birthday I opted against jew-

ellery after I was still mentally limping from the drain incident. After much discussion, we somewhat democratically decided that with my £10 budget (more than a week's wages on my paper round before you start rolling your eyes) I would get her a Samantha Mumba CD from Sclaters. A shop that sold pipes, lightbulbs, floor tiles, paint, hammers and for some reason CDs. It also carried a name which, to be fair to Word processor, even I would underline with an aggressive red line because it looks wrong no matter how accurate the spelling is. Anyway, so I got her that CD, wrapped it up (not sure why I bothered with this part to be honest when she was fully aware what it was, and the paper took me over my strict and clearly set out budget.) She was happy enough, as someone that had just received a Samantha Mumba CD could be. The next day she told me her dad didn't approve of me because he felt that by getting her a CD I was taking things too seriously, and it was moving far too fast. Three months or so in, we hadn't even kissed, barely made eye contact and had only recently graduated to the awkwardly holding hands stage in proceedings, but as soon as a CD exchanges hands, it's off to the convent and don't pass go. This would be the ideal part in the narrative to shoehorn in a Samantha Mumba song, but as we've already established, that's copyright, so I can't.

Things didn't really last long after that, partly through fear of her mysterious ninja assassin dad (never met the guy, but got that sort of vibe) and partly because things sort of just ran their course as most early high school relationships do.

Last I heard she left school quite early and had a child, which on listening back to the album (for research purposes as the guy from The Who would say...) the singer strongly advised against both of those scenarios in her smash-hit single 'Body 2 Body.'

Her dad probably wouldn't appreciate the butterfly effect irony of confiscating that Samantha Mumba CD.

SKATEBOARDING:

Christmas 2001's equivalent of Tracy Island was a skateboard. If upon returning to school early January you weren't sporting grazes and bullshit tales of a 360 reverse kickflip down a set of stairs that went wrong then you were branded a term I was previously unfamiliar with. A Ned. The definition of a Ned was essentially someone that wore a tracksuit and Lynx Africa combo and beat up anything that dare make accidental eye contact with their shadow (I say beat up anything, and I mean anything- I once witnessed a gentleman on Leith Walk in Edinburgh decked out in full cotton Adidas regalia aim several missed punches in the direction of the sun) The tracksuit part was baffling at first, as less than 2 years prior to Ned-gate, tracksuits were the order of the day. By early 2002, my beloved Lecoq Sportif tracksuit was to be banished to the back of the wardrobe and deep into retirement in *Narnia*, never to be seen again. It would be replaced by baggy jeans, hoodies and oversized DC shoes. With this change also came a drastic change in music as I'd mentioned earlier. *Now 44* no longer seemed a safe option to have on within earshot of anyone from school, so in came a truckload of new bands, some of whom I liked, others I merely put up with in order to create the illusion that I had a vague idea I knew what the fuck I was doing in my early teens. I did love skateboarding, though, like most of my hobbies, I wasn't very good at it.

I spent many a summer holiday in Peebles from dawn to dusk desperately trying to nail down anything other than an ollie (a reasonably basic trick where you would flick the board up in the air and land straight back down) in an attempt to compete with my seemingly professional mates in order to gain some valuable and highly sought after street cred- to no avail. Don't get me wrong, I had the art of skating around in a straight line down to a tee. Tricks wise though I was the skateboarding equivalent of David Blaine-when he did nothing but shit in a glass box suspended above the Thames for forty-four days and expected people to be amazed by his efforts.

EXAMS/CHEATING DEATH:

Exams were a bit of a shock to the system. In theory, having done endless amounts of revision, it should have been plain sailing. The slight drawback of my revision style was that most of it was ineffective procrastination. I'd get home from school, grab a cup of tea and then set up my desk for a night's worth of what I rather inaccurately referred to as "exam preparation." I struggled to fully, or even partially immerse myself in the nonsense that lay before me. I'd open a biology book-then immediately close it as the scent of decade's worth of dust, dissected fish eyes and boredom was too strong for me to stomach. I'd begrudgingly open a Maths book, look at the numbers then think to myself 'nobody ever needs to know this pish.' Then I'd pick up a calculator, type 58008, turn it upside down and chuckle a bit, before taking a well-deserved hour long break while I watched *Neighbours* and *The Simpsons*. Two hours later (it was a long walk) I'd return to my desk, stare blankly into space for a bit and then pack my bag for the following day. For a while, I thought it was near impossible for me to revise. My brain was always too busy installing updates any time I tried to learn something important instead of retaining any key information. I later found out when studying Music Business at college that it was surprisingly effortless to learn and retain information when it was a subject that actually interested me. The problem was, nothing ever really sufficiently caught my interest at school. Oddly enough, in a rather fortunate turn of events, and something I continue to take great pleasure in telling people; not studying saved my life. On paper (or Kindle, whatever medium you're reading this on) it's not exactly the most dramatic of the "saved my life" series. You see some crazy ones on *Mail Online* like 'Hispanic David Beckham lookalike fends off bloodthirsty badger to save my life.' Or 'My brother's imaginary friend saved my life from near-fatal three-tier cake avalanche at my uncle's third wedding.' This one doesn't really have a decent ring to it, but it was genuinely a pretty horrible experience.

One April or May, I was due to be revising, probably for my doomed French exam, which I'll mention in a moment. This was massively important, and after several crisis talks with my Mum and Dad about my lack of effort in the revising department, I had assured them that I would do my best to pick my socks up and they need not worry as 'It will all be fine by the exams mes parents.' This really was last chance saloon for me to wing something that would narrowly resemble a grade.

This was it.one first and final push. It was now or never.

Anyway, needless to say, I was not studying. I was embroiled in a very important quarter-final tie of the Konami Cup or something in *Pro Evolution Soccer 3*. If you're not familiar with the *Pro Evo* series, many believed it to be better than *FIFA*, but the deal breaker for hardened football fans was the lack of licensed teams. So whilst I, playing as Manchester United had a crunch tie against fierce rivals Manchester City, for legal reasons the game would refer to their non-licensed names of Trad Bricks (United) against Lloyd (City). Doesn't really have 'too important to study' game written all over it. To be fair though, it could have been a Scotland v Scotland exhibition match and I still would have deemed it too important a game to let studying intervene like some unwanted streaker. After all, I owed those pixelated fans a game of football (or five.) Midway through an unscripted and unusually sluggish performance from the imposters in red, I heard an almighty crash.

'...piss, I should probably pause it' and 'is it my formation or the players' fitness that's letting me down?' ran through my head simultaneously as I downed tools and went for an inspection. I wandered down the hall and into my living room to see a room full of dust. As the dust cloud began to separate, I could see a big hole in the ceiling and large chunks of concrete covering the piano and the desk which would normally house my poor excuse for studying. My heart sank as next to the desk, Skye would usually sleep and bathe in the sunlight. Luckily she was in the hallway and like me was extremely fortunate to narrowly avoid a Pompeii makeover. What happened was that the part of the roof that fell in was located directly beneath the flat roof/ balcony which belonged to the upstairs neighbours and it had dried out so much that it caused part of the roof to cave in. It could have been much worse, and luckily there was nothing that couldn't be fixed. Having said that, I never got to finish that game of *Pro Evo*.

The Standard Grade French exam of 2004 was a particularly low point for my academic achievements (or lack of.) The exam unfortunately coincided with muck up day. Muck up day at school was a bit like transfer deadline day on Sky Sports. Built up massively each year, only to end up being complete pish. For those of you unfamiliar with the concept, it was the last day of school for the sixth year students- a day in which they promised in no uncertain terms to cause anarchy in the school. The head teacher was particularly wary about it because a year or two before someone had put red food colouring in the pond to make it look like blood- this inadvertently killed all of the fish in the pond and the heads quite rightly went ballistically ape-shit about it. Not a lot had happened in 2004's instalment- until the boringly predictable fire alarm went off. As you can imagine, this isn't the best thing that could have happened a mere thirty minutes prior to an exam. The whole 1000 strong school trundled out to the playing field to "anxiously" await further instruction of when we could go back in. The fire drill had been going off for a good half hour when it was decided we would play football in the field across the road. The plan was simple, play football until the alarm goes off, then hurry back in and knock my French exam out of the park and walk out feeling like a Peebles version of Zinedine Zidane. After an early goal, I was brimming with confidence- that was until the alarm unexpectedly went off. I gathered my bag and hurried back into the building. Only to be greeted by the French teacher at the door to the hall who sympathetically advised that the exam was about to start and I was too late. I went home and broke the news to my Mum that I scored a great goal, and slipped in the footnote of the story that I missed the exam. The merits of the goal were arguably somewhat cruelly omitted when the tale was retold to my Dad later that evening. Still, all wasn't lost- I managed to appeal and was awarded a grade three which I'd been diagnosed with after underperforming in my prelims a few months before. Still, peach of a goal though and it lived long in the memory more than any of my French lingo that I'd managed to accidentally sieve clean out of my brain.

ON THE ROAD:

Driving is one of those things, like flying whereby I'm too caught up in the notion that I'm going to die each time I'm in the seat to enjoy it that much. I was never one of those instantly confident boy racer types that used to burn petrol circling the two hundred metre stretch of Peebles High Street in search of someone that didn't think they were an arsehole. I fell into the other bracket, the terrified, low on self-confidence, high on driving errors types.

On my first lesson, the instructor nearly ended up in tears as I blitzed my way through a white van's wing mirror like some sort of deranged caffeine-fuelled slalom skier. He retired not long after that, safe in the knowledge that he wouldn't have to be a passenger with brakes that did bugger all to stop a mad man crashing into some poor soul's wing mirrors again.

The theory test was hard work and took me a good three attempts to pass. The added incentive to pass on my third attempt was so I didn't have to be on the receiving end of another unbearably awkward sympathy stare from the old guy that ran the test centre when he was tasked with delivering the bad news.

If coasting was one of the test manoeuvres, I'd have fucking nailed the test on the first attempt. Unfortunately for me, it appeared this was generally frowned upon, and so I hung up my L plates for another few years until I felt ready to get back behind the wheel again. More on that in the next instalment (if that's not enough incentive to buy Part Two, don't worry, there's plenty more shameless promotion to come in the closing pages.)

A NEW DAWN:

High school became a more comfortable and happier place to be when the majority of my enemies left school at sixteen in order to pursue other avenues; like getting a trade, parenthood or the young offenders institute. There was undoubtedly much less tiptoeing on eggshells around the school grounds, and that brought about a certain sense of confidence that I hadn't really discovered before. I was hardly Mr Popular around the place, swanning around like I was in *Grease*- far from it- but I without a doubt enjoyed it much more than I had thought possible in the first three years there. Of course this wasn't solely down to the fact that a few shady characters had left, that just triggered me to feel more comfortable around the place and far more at ease with my surroundings- a feeling shared with others around the place, who too seemed to loosen the tie a bit, settle in and relax a bit more.

Around the end of fifth year, I started to become a little uneasy at something that the school had failed miserably to get me to focus on for years. That one word that's great if you put *'Back to the'* in front of it but far less exciting and worryingly less plausible when you put 'my' in front of it. That's right-Future. The word that when uttered immediately makes you avoid all manner of eye contact and causes you to run in the opposite direction towards the nearest brick wall. What was such a nightmare about it was that before, I'd see people taking three Advanced Higher sciences and think 'pah, silly wankers!' Then it became abundantly clear that they'd actually planned out what they wanted to do in later life, or at least when they left school. I went through an endless amount of computer programmes in social education that gave a hollow promise that it would be able to find my "dream job" by the third time of it suggesting armed forces I became understandably suspicious and disillusioned with its shite and inaccurate selection process. At least at the age of five, I had realistic aspirations of being a bin man in an orange truck. I can't recall that option being available on the high school's computer programme. With the worry cloud of my future hovering over me, I felt it was essential to pick sensible options for what to study (obviously I use that term loosely) for the forthcoming last year of high school. With that in mind, I chose sensibly. I took a crash Higher in Drama... My thought process was that so long as they didn't paint me green and put baubles on my fingers again then it could be considered a resounding success and arguably in a way a clear sign of career progression. Aside from the distractingly beautiful female classmates, the highlight was that I successfully managed to rip off an Oasis video when writing an acting piece for the class. I even had the tenacity to use the name of the accompanying song 'The Importance of Being Idle' as the name of my short play. The concept was the main cast member was at a funeral and then slowly pegged that it was actually her own and she was dead the whole time. I dubbed it a budget, more convincing version of *The Sixth Sense*. Nobody agreed. Long story short, I passed the acting part with flying colours ("skin of your teeth" was the official term generously given from my teacher, but I think she was just trying to keep my feet on the ground) the written part though, I heroically ballsed up because I wasn't able to justify anything about my acting (or anyone else's) on paper. My one-way ticket to Hollywood was in tatters. So it was a good job I had a reasonable backup plan...

ROCK STAR:

The high school charity concert was, for a lot of people, a platform in which to showcase yourself in front of a total of around 1000 people in the hope that masses would suddenly realise your hidden talent. Unfortunately for some people, the hidden talent remained hidden for the entirety of their performance. This was particularly uneasy viewing when some young aspiring singers or musicians took to the stage as when the curtain went up, they would hold their nerve about as well as they'd hold their opening note. On that note (or lack of) in one final push for relevance and recognition in high school, I decided to throw my hat in the ring. Being somewhat limited at guitar at that point, I decided to play the rather simplistic 'United States of Whatever' by Liam Lynch. The acts that year were primarily arranged into two categories-deadly serious or complete piss take. My act suffered in that nobody, myself included really knew what it was. Though my Green Day-inspired black shirt and red tie suggested I was taking this all a bit too seriously. I can't remember too much going wrong other than during the second performance when I threw my plectrum out into the by that point mildly disorientated crowd, only for a girl in the front row to gasp, followed up by my boomerang like plectrum to circle the first two rows and land back on stage as the curtains were closing on my performance and continued pursuit of fame. Though I wouldn't call it a particularly great success, by any stretch of the imagination, it did leave me hungry for more gigs as there was something special about playing to a room full of people, even if the majority didn't have even the slightest idea what to make of it.

Whatever.

THE BEGINNING
OF THE END:

After Christmas in my final year of school, the screw began to tighten and it felt as though there was an almost 1984-esque approach from the school towards further education and more specifically university. It was becoming near impossible to continue to bury my head in the sand whenever the 'U' word was mentioned. In my eyes, it felt like the stage was set for others to star and grab their future whilst I was still floundering up the top in the cheap seats awaiting a spotlight to shine on me that I knew fine well wouldn't arrive. If you want another analogy, imagine I was the one with tap hands waiting at the side of the gym hall for an injury substitution whilst others were ready to start 'The Canadian Barn Dance.' Over-thinking and under-doing was and continues to be my Achilles heel. Perfect example being that even as I was writing the last few sentences down just then, I stood up with the intent to make a cup of coffee three times without so much as even boiling the kettle before returning to complete the paragraph.

Backed into a corner, I applied for a few courses I thought looked vaguely interesting. The universities I did apply for, on paper seemed obtainable. I went for the margherita pizza of university courses, Events Management. A course that I know at least sixty percent of my Twitter friends studied because they insist on having a god awful tag line of 'Events Management Grad. Looking to book more gigs soon. Tea drinker.' They and I both know that there's about as much chance of them putting on another gig as there is someone finding their mention of tea in any way relevant or endearing. The condition of getting into these universities was that I got another three Highers. With these offers on the table, you would be forgiven for thinking a switch might flick and I'd suddenly up my game. The problem was, the tide was coming in a lot quicker than I'd anticipated and I wasn't doing a very good job of fixing my shipwrecked boat that was full of holes. Whilst it was clear my focus should have been on achieving the necessary grades in order to breathe a sigh of relief, instead, enjoying what little time I had left of high school took a front seat.

The last few months were great, not least because I'd managed to enjoy a brief relationship which trumped the others I'd had up until that point. It was all seemingly going brilliantly until the inevitable grim reaper of relationships turned up unexpectedly one fateful Tuesday afternoon. I remember the pain of the unexpected breakup being on a similar level to waking up one morning to a note from my sister Gemma many years before advising me that she'd accidentally prematurely killed my Tamagotchi after what, by all accounts felt like it had been the happiest four days of our(the Tamagotchi and I's) lives. The note ended with the tragic words of 'but it probably would have died anyway.' A torturously accurate line that could quite easily have made the headstone of many of my first few doomed lessons in love. If someone (I.e., Gemma) had reminded me of Tamagotchi-gate, perhaps I would have seen the similarities between the untimely and short-lived acquaintances and not spent the rest of the summer being melodramatic. Either that or I'd have been doubly depressed upon receipt of the insensitive and poorly timed reminder. As for the exams... To cut a long story short, I Hibsed my exams and only got one more Higher which wasn't enough. What had in many ways been the best year I'd had in my thirteen years of education had ended on a sour note. I was fairly gutted about this in the sense that I, now more than ever had no idea what I was going to do next. Prior to that, my big decisions would consist of trying to figure out what I'd do with my weekends, or free time in the summer holidays, not my whole life. I should have probably cottoned on to this eventuality two years previously, but I had more trivial things to worry about then like spots or what band names I'd scribble on my bag to appear relevant. The safety net of education was no longer there, so I really had to buck up my ideas and make some lifestyle choices. Until then, I'd go to T in the Park. (Actually, that bits a lie. I did go to T in the Park, but I've just remembered that my exam results arrived around a month after T in the park so I can't have known I'd failed the lion's share of my exams at that point. Let's just say given my previous track record and the multiple centimetres squared of blank space I'd left on many of the pages, I had more than a hunch on the outcome.) I'd first experienced Scotland's former biggest music festival the year before in 2005. The headliners that year were Green Day and The Foo Fighters (I opted to see James Brown in the King Tut's tent instead, and I'm still genuinely surprised and proud I made that choice. It was far and wide my best decision that weekend, though upon reflection I'm hardly spoilt for choice in that regard.) I turned up with no tent, no alcohol and no clue what to expect. My knowledge of music festivals up until then relied on what I'd seen on *Hollyoaks* where the characters would come back from Leeds in a bucket hat, still tripping their balls off unscripted a week later- whilst in the narrative of the show, suffering from a mild overdose of Strepsils. My only other source of information came again from the tv, but this time from an advert for Daz or some other washing powder. The dishevelled forty-year-old son would return home, again bucket hat in tow and immediately, avoid red-eye contact with his oddly posh mother before uttering his fully deserved £70 line of "Glastonbury." Before curling up in the foetal position on the couch. As soon as his eyes were clamped shut, his mum did what any other caring mother in her position would go. Grossly invaded her son's privacy and raided his backpack like a police dog high on Winalot. The camera slowly pans in on her face which is whiter than the Daz itself, like it's a shower scene in *Psycho*. Poor guy, she must have found his Glastonbury washing up powder which he valiantly tried to hide. Nope, she's found a white shirt covered in second-hand bolognese. A trend I arguably pioneered in the early '90s I might add. (This was a thirty second advert by the way even though I'm drawing it out like it's *Lawrence of Arabia*). Festivals must have taken this on board though after hundreds of complaints from despondent parents about the bolognese stains that ruined their angel's shirts and they'd never be the same again as a result, because I didn't see anyone selling bolognese once that weekend. Unlike the previous year, in 2006 I was able to buy alcohol risk-free, as were the majority of my friends, so we no longer relied on carefully choreographing our friend and saviour Rob into walking and talking like an eighteen-year-old in order to fool the poor old guy behind the counter that the ninety-six cans of Tennents and eight bottles of cider he purchased were for personal consumption. I can't remember who I saw headline that year, though I do remember missing The Who in favour of a band in the Futures tent because I was so drunk I thought I was being forward thinking and it would be a funny story back in the campsite. It wasn't.

Living in the live music apocalypse of the Borders and being an infrequent gig goer up until my first few festivals, T in the Park was a portal to a new and exciting world where hundreds of bands were on my doorstep for the first time. Up until then, local bands nights were one of the only opportunities to see a band in what felt like the music prohibition capital of Scotland. Bands night consisted of three or four mixed bag bands from the high school playing covers to an audience who were all suitably inebriated having indulged in the pre-gig delights of half a bottle of Lambrini between about twenty giddy teenagers with varying levels of facial expression consisting of either extreme happiness at hearing 'Smells Like Teen Spirit' badly done three times in the same evening or being part of the one hiccup away from projectile vomiting crew who always seemed to turn up in strong numbers at these things. Regardless of quality, people were just excited to see live music in Peebles (or they were just excited because they were absolutely off their tits.) The one time I remember seeing a band that you could argue actual constituted a touring band (they had a van, so it definitely counts) in Peebles, I was buzzing. I don't think I even resented paying something in the dizzy heights region of £10 for a ticket from the tourist information shop I was that excited. "The best Black Sabbath tribute band in Scotland." The poster read "Crikey; these guys must be the real deal, this will probably sell out in minutes" I remember saying to best mate and occasional Arsenal fan, Euan who I convinced to go along. There was surely no way that Mac Sabbath were going to disappoint... Up first that night was the imaginatively titled 'Das Rainbow' who surprise, surprise were a Rainbow tribute band. My only prior knowledge of *Rainbow* was that it was a tv show and Zippy ruled the roost. Apparently this wasn't a tribute to the tv show, more to the band of the same name that only those sporting two items of denim or more seemed to have any clue about. I didn't take much away from their set other than an overbearing feeling that they were taking the piss and a song and a half in I was wishing they were a tribute to the tv show so that someone could do the decent thing and zip the frontman's mouth shut. My hope was momentarily restored when the pot of gold finally arrived in the form of the end of their set, some thirty or forty minutes later, little did I know that things were somehow going to get a lot worse. The first tell-tale sign that something was afoot was that nothing was rolled off the stage to be replaced with Mac Sabbath's gear. This set alarm bells off in the audience. Now, having built this gig up more than the promoter, my disappointment was signed, sealed and attempting to be delivered, I just wasn't answering the door yet in case I was mistaken. "Surely not? I mean they couldn't possibly be the... oh for fu..." At that moment Das Rainbow reappeared for an unwanted encore, this time sporting all-black attire and different wigs, which the singer still appeared to be affixing as he was staggering across the stage. The penny eventually dropped from the gravity of false hope that had been levitating it off the floor; "Euan mate, I think Mac Sabbath and Das Rainbow are the same band." Was said with about as much guilt, embarrassment, contempt and horror as Hillary Clinton's speech when conceding defeat to Donald Trump. Though at least Donald Trump probably had enough restraint not to stand in front of her doing bad karaoke, wearing an oversized crucifix fashioned from Tesco value tinfoil whilst charging £10 for the honour. Maybe I shouldn't have been as disappointed at how much of a colossal let down that gig was, what with Peebles being starved of live music. The family that opened the shoe-box with the black eyed beans in it were presumably in a similar rock and a hard place with their disappoint-ment.

Back to T in the Park, for many, music took a back seat that weekend with the campsite being where they would spend eighty percent of their time, much to their livers dismay. Whilst the mad debauchery of the campsite was great fun; there was no disguising that my main intentions that weekend were to see as many bands as possible. I treated the festival like a wine tast-ing, I'd literally try anything that was in front of me. If I didn't like it, I'd just not go back for more and if I con-sumed enough, I'd probably forget about the shite ones. I discovered lots of my favourite bands by chance see-ing them play in front of twelve people in a small tent whilst nursing a broken amplifier or narrowly avoiding electrocution during one of the weekend's infamous rainstorms. I witnessed one of my favourite bands, The Horrors walk on stage with the lead singer wearing a cape, eyeballing the crowd and carrying a pineapple on a rope over his right shoulder before spending the ma-jority of the frantic twenty-minute set trying to knock down the disco ball that was suspended high above the stage with his microphone. If only he'd used the pine-apple he'd have probably smashed it in a oner. These are the things I remember at the festival, more than big-name touring bands who are month seventeen into their eighteen-month tour of the same songs and really can't be arsed.

After writing that bit, I stopped writing the book for six months, something I could just brush off as writer's block. But it wasn't writer's block- it's almost impossible to suffer from writer's block when you're writing about your own life, unless you're Keith Richards or the guy that played *Harry Potter* as he'd been smashing the vodka through every orifice when filming so fortunately for him he managed to forget about most of those films ever existing. Like I was saying, it wasn't writer's block, my lack of creativity was down to the fact that I didn't have a particularly great few years after that and it's unpleasant to think about, let alone write about. Nothing particularly bad happened, it was just a bit of a downer in comparison to the years before them. I recall being really mopey and not a lot of laughs that summer, partly due to the break-up (Coldplay had probably released another sad song at that point) and partly down to my lack of forward planning. This was another classic example of all too often collecting small pebbles of disappointment and instead of throwing them away, I'd hoard them, wade out to the middle of the sea with them and wonder why I was feeling vulnerable, a bit lost and struggling to keep afloat. I'm still just as bad for that really, I'll subconsciously default to being down in the dumps and feeling sorry for myself for a situation that deep down I know isn't the end of the world, but that'll be enough for me to sufficiently lose focus that I won't solve it, I'll just needlessly dwell.

A lifeline was thrown by my Dad late that summer as he'd managed to pull a few strings to get me enrolled last minute on a course at Napier University in Edinburgh, studying Building Surveying. Admittedly, this wasn't a course I'd had in mind, far from it, but I was nonetheless ecstatic at the unexpected news as it meant I could live the student lifestyle and defer needing to think about what I was wanting to do with my life for another four years.

That was the plan anyway...

...That was going to be the end of Part One, but having read back over the last few lines it's awfully whiny and doesn't really help my case for promoting a second one of these, so instead, I'll hand you a brief kaleidoscope into what goes down in Part Two.

- I terminate my contract with university after one year of my four-year contract to explore other options. I.e., fucking anything else.

- I try my hand at stand-up comedy but forget to invite the audience to laugh.
- I crash a car on Valentine's Day. Both meta-phorically and literally.
- I have a brief unexpected fling with a delayed goth phase.
- I interview David Hasselhoff.
- I move to Australia for a bit.

- I write about two-thirds of a book, don't finish it so decide to release it in two parts to attempt to give myself a much-needed kick up the arse to finish it and to double up on the profits as they did with the last *Twilight* film.
- I likely get sued by at least one person for something in Part One, probably the fireplace shop.

Oh and one more thing, I watched *Blue Planet* tonight, and I want to save the wee sad looking seals and turtles, so if you were kind enough to buy this on paperback, can you please be equally kind and recycle your copy instead of throwing it in the direction of a bin man in an orange truck, tempting as that may be. If you bought the Kindle version, double delete should do the trick.

-End of Part One- Please insert Part Two here

--------------->

41164894R00085

Printed in Poland
by Amazon Fulfillment
Poland Sp. z o.o., Wrocław